Bootstrap Quick Start

Supports Bootstrap 4.2.1

Learning web development is a lot more challenging than it used to be.

Responsive web design adds more layers of complexity to design and develop websites. In this book you will become familiar with the new cards component, setting up the new flexbox grid layout, customizing the look and feel, how to follow the mobile-first development workflow, and more!

This book does not duplicate what you can already find in the official documentation but instead shows you how to reference the documentation and use it effectively in your projects to save time.

**Learn How to Build a Marketing Site
and an Admin Dashboard... Step by Step.**

Also includes access to a recorded training video on responsive design basics.
See page 26 for details.

*The training documents were great and **got me started quickly**. I was able to jump into getting my website framework started.*

—— *Andrew Diaz, web developer new to Bootstrap*

*It is clear and well structured. **A good start for Bootstrap 4 beginners.***

—— *Uwe, web developer beginner*

Bootstrap 4 Quick Start

Copyright © 2019 by Jacob Lett | Published on January 1, 2019

Publisher

Bootstrap Creative | Sterling Heights, Michigan 48314 | (586) 894-8024
To report errors, please send an email to support@bootstrapcreative.com
Find us on the web at: bootstrapcreative.com

Notice of Rights

Notice of Liability

Trademarks

ISBN: 978-1-7322058-1-9

Contents

Dedicated to my wife Colleen.

Thank you for your persistent love and encouragement.

Thank you!

I would like to thank the following for their advice and support with this project: Greg Vance, Dan Joseph, Max, and my encouraging parents. Marcus and Joshua thank you for your patience as your Dad was working on this project. Also my mentors for their wisdom and inspiration: Zig Ziglar, Dan Miller, Seth Godin, and Matthew 25:14-30.

Finally, thank you reader for purchasing this book.
My hope is to help you be successful in your web development projects and career.

About the Author

Jacob Lett is the author of the *Bootstrap 4 Quick Start*, and the *Bootstrap Reference Guide*. His books and training help web developers save time learning how to design and build responsive websites.
www.linkedin.com/in/jacoblett/

Introduction

Do you remember learning how to write a research paper?

Perhaps you learned how to follow the MLA or APA Style Guide.

Think how different the reports would look if each student made up their own style and format?

Using the MLA Style guaranteed consistency for anyone who followed that same format even if they were thousands of miles away or written five years apart.

I believe Bootstrap works the same way for web design. It helps developers work more efficiently and write CSS in a clean and consistent manner regardless of where you live or who you work for.

It also ensures your website adheres to a mobile first approach and works well across browsers and devices.

I am convinced Bootstrap will greatly improve how you build websites and save you countless time. So if you're ready, let's get started.

Hi.

My name is Jacob Lett and it's my mission to help you save time learning how to design and build responsive websites.

I earned a bachelors degree in graphic design around the time CSS
and web standards were just starting to take hold. Out of frustration
not knowing how to fix broken websites generated by Dreamweaver,
I learned how to hand code HTML/CSS. Then in 2009 I got my first job
as a web designer writing a ton of CSS and realizing I had a long journey
of learning ahead.

in www.linkedin.com/in/jacoblett/

Initial Setup

Before we begin, we need to make sure you have all of the necessary software and tools installed on your computer. So let's get started.

1. Install Google Chrome

I recommend testing your sites in Google Chrome because of their nice set of DevTools to help you debug problems and inspect CSS styles and HTML elements. If you do not have this it installed you can do so here[1].

In my *Bootstrap 4 Toolkit,* [2] I include a tutorial video titled *Inspect and Test CSS* that demonstrates how to use Chrome DevTools.

2. Install Chrome Extensions

These are optional but very helpful.

live.js Extension

Install the live.js Chrome extension[3] to toggle the ability to automatically reload your browser when you make code changes. Or you can manually add the script found at http://livejs.com/.

Web Developer Extension

Install the Web Developer Chrome extension[4] to help you test responsive breakpoints and perform other developer focused tasks.

---

1   https://www.google.com/chrome/browser/desktop/index.html
2   http://bootstrapcreative.com/b4toolkit
3   https://bootstrapcreative.com/livejschrome
4   https://bootstrapcreative.com/webdevchrome

3. Setup a Local Testing Server

If you are new to web servers, a local server is on your desktop/laptop and a remote server is located someplace else accessible via SFTP. Web servers are just big computers with software installed for the sole purpose of hosting websites and data. The benefit of having a local test server is you can eliminate the step of transferring changed files to a remote server and avoid the public seeing your unfinished work.

The easiest way to start testing sites locally is using a tool called XAMPP on windows or MAMP on a mac. It lets you run PHP, apache, and even phpMyAdmin for MySQL database configuration. Commonly referred to as the LAMP web stack[5] of bundled software.

Windows

Install XAMPP[6] following the instructions in this guide. It is written for WordPress users so you can ignore the part of setting up a database and installing WordPress. You want the ability to make HTTP requests (or access files on other servers). I created this video tutorial[7] on how to install XAMPP on Windows 10.

---

5   https://en.wikipedia.org/wiki/LAMP_(software_bundle)

6   https://www.apachefriends.org/index.html

7   https://bootstrapcreative.com/installxampp

Mac

Install MAMP[8] following the instructions in this guide. It is written for WordPress users so you can ignore the part of setting up a database and installing WordPress. You want the ability to make HTTP requests (or access files on other servers).

Linux

Install Mongoose Binary[9]. A really light weight server ideal for web design testing.

4. Install a Code Text Editor

Install a code text editor so you can benefit from code syntax coloring and other features that make the job of writing code easier. There are a lot of editors available and it comes down to your preference.

I personally use Visual Studio Code because it's free, cross platform, and works really well without having to add a lot of addons.

Below are some other popular code editors available:

- **Atom** (free, cross platform): https://atom.io/
- **Brackets** (free, cross platform): http://brackets.io/
- **Dreamweaver** (paid, cross platform): http://www.adobe.com/products/dreamweaver.html
- **Notepad++** (free, Windows only): https://notepad-plus-plus.org/download/v7.3.3.html
- **TextWrangler** (free, mac only): http://www.barebones.com/products/textwrangler/download.html
- **Visual Studio Code** (free, cross platform): https://code.visualstudio.com/
- **Other editors:** https://en.wikipedia.org/wiki/Source_code_editor#Some_well-known_source_code_editors

---

8   https://bootstrapcreative.com/installmamp
9   https://www.cesanta.com/products/binary

5. Mobile First Desktop Workspace

Next, open up your Chrome web browser then press **F12** to open Chrome DevTools. Next, press **CTRL + SHIFT + D** (win) or **CMD + SHIFT + D** (mac) to move the dock to the right side of your browser window.

Reference for all of Chrome DevTools shortcuts: https://developers.google.com/web/tools/chrome-devtools/shortcuts

Then move your text editor window to the left half of your screen and your browser to the right half of your screen using the keyboard shortcuts **WIN + ➜** and **WIN + ←** (win) you will need to adjust the windows manually on a mac.

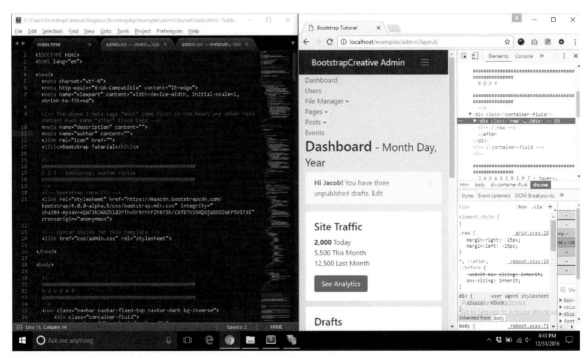

Start coding/testing mobile first - *Your screen should now look like this.*

Get FREE Bootstrap Reference Sheets

Includes the following three references:

Bootstrap 4 Cheat Sheet | Flexbox Cheat Sheet | CSS3 Cheat Sheet

https://bootstrapcreative.com/b4bundle

The Mobile Web & Bootstrap

Building websites today is a lot more challenging and time consuming than it used to be.

Some of my first websites were first designed in Adobe Photoshop,® exported to HTML tables (yes tables) and then linked together with Adobe Dreamweaver.® If your website did not exceed the width of common monitor resolutions (1024px by 768px) everything would work out fine.

Web standards[1] were quickly introduced because using table markup for grid layout is just bad practice. So HTML tables were replaced with floated divs and tag markup that had meaning – referred to as semantics. This also shifted things away from the majority of the visual design being baked into images and now relying on CSS3 to create borders, shadows, rounded corners, etc.

The first widely used CSS grid system was the 960 grid system (Fig. 1) created by Nathan Smith. This 12,16, 24 column grid system was designed to work well for a fixed desktop resolution of 1024px x 768px. This grid system was widely used and helped designers and developers work from the same grid pixel dimensions.

Fig. 1: The 960 grid system helped bring consistency between grid design in Photoshop and the web.

---

1   https://www.goodreads.com/book/show/259072.Designing_With_Web_Standards

Then in 2007, Steve Jobs introduced the world to the iPhone with Multi-Touch gestures[2]. Now people could access websites anywhere using just their fingers.

Web designers and developers had to quickly develop creative solutions to work within the new constraints presented by smartphones and tablets.

These Constraints Include:

- Smaller screens
- Increased pixel densities with retina displays
- Ability to switch between portrait and landscape orientation
- Multi-touch gestures
- Slower data connections
- Distracted user attention (one eyeball and one thumb).

At the start, the concept of responsive design did not exist. And so mobile devices had to scale down websites to fit the smaller screens. For the user, in order to read the text they would have to double tap the screen or pinch and zoom.

Website owners quickly realized it was not a good experience to display their homepage at a zoomed in level. The meta tag below was introduced to remove this default scaling and give the site creator more control. When this meta tag is added to the <head> of a page, it instructs the web browser to scale the document 100% to prevent pinch/zoom on mobile.

```
<meta name="viewport" content="width=device-width, initial-scale=1">
```

---

2   http://www.lukew.com/ff/entry.asp?1071

Different Mobile Strategies

Mobile Applications

One approach is to build a dedicated experience as a mobile app. This gives the developer the most control and could utilize the device user interface components and to help with navigation. Major drawbacks include: it requires an app developer, considerable amount of marketing to direct existing traffic to download the mobile app, and overcoming low rates of user adoption. Also, any links to outside pages required them to open in a web browser window.

Adaptive Design

Another approach is to build multiple versions of a website and use server side detection to then present custom code for that device or viewport size.

You could decide to have your mobile site on a separate domain for example m.domain. com. The server will then automatically serve all mobile traffic to that domain. The server could also perform dynamic serving of page content so that you have just one domain name. The downsides to this approach is it requires complex server side detection code and is harder to maintain multiple site versions.

Responsive Design

Responsive design was introduced to help designers build one site on one domain that responds to a users viewport. The two necessary elements for a responsive design are a meta viewport tag to disable scaling and media queries to alter the design as the page gets smaller. Responsive design is a lot less expensive and easier to maintain than the other mobile strategies. This has added to its rapid growth and adoption.

A big challenge with responsive design is finding a balance between the content needs for both mobile and desktop. A desktop site has a lot of visual real estate that is often filled with carousels, videos, large parallax background images, and large blocks of text.

If you load a feature-rich website on a mobile device you often increase the page load for mobile visitors. This is due to the large images and videos which are scaled down to mobile.

End-users don't care about your responsive web or your separate sites, **they just want to be able to get stuff done quickly.**

— Brad Frost, author of Atomic Design

Mobile First

In the desktop first approach, you sacrifice the mobile experience because you have a lot of images and text content. In an article from Zurb on mobile first design it said, "Roughly 80% of the screen size is taken away when you start with mobile first design, you have to think about how to utilize your space in a much more conservative manner."

Fig. 2 - Desktop First Responsive Site

	Desktop	**Mobile**
Data Speed	Fast	Slow
Width	Wide	Narrow
Height	Unlimited	Unlimited
Retina Display Probability	Medium	High
Page File Size	Large	Large

A mobile first approach considers the goals of a mobile user and presents the content to help them achieve those goals. It removes all of the fluff and filler content and presents a concise collection of content that loads fast and is easy to use.

Fig 3. Mobile First Responsive Site

	Mobile	Desktop
Data Speed	Slow	Fast
Width	Narrow	Wide
Height	Unlimited	Unlimited
Retina Display Probability	High	Medium
Page File Size	Small	Medium +

The chart above shows the workflow flipped so the site is built mobile first and then enhancements are added as the viewport gets wider. Notice how the mobile site is loading a small file size on a slow data speed? That is as Google would say, being mobile friendly.

But some might say. "Ok now the mobile site looks good but now the desktop looks too basic and lacks flair."

Progressive Enhancement

A great way to solve this is to progressively enhance the page as your data speed and screen width increases. Everything you add to the page will be enhancing the design and if it doesn't load for some reason your page is still usable.

> *Screens are small, connections are slow, and people often only give you their partial attention or short bursts of their time.* **Designing for mobile first forces you to embrace these constraints**
>
> —— *Luke Wroblewski, Mobile First*

The best way to do this is with JavaScript media queries[3] to determine viewport width and then load in content to the page. I created a small plugin called IfBreakpoint.js[4] to help detect Bootstrap 4 breakpoints with JavaScript. I also recommend reading this article[5] on ways to progressively load images with media queries.

One creative solution that has transformed the web and made responsive design easier for web designers has been the Bootstrap frontend framework. We will take a closer look at Bootstrap in the next section.

---

3   https://jacoblett.github.io/IfBreakpoint/
4   https://jacoblett.github.io/IfBreakpoint/
5   https://timkadlec.com/2012/04/media-query-asset-downloading-results/

What is Bootstrap?

I remember building my first few responsive websites. I wasted so much time writing the same type of styles over and over for each new project. I also found it difficult to find plugins that worked well together and had cohesive design style

I then heard about Bootstrap and I liked how it included javascript components and had really comprehensive documentation. The documentation was extremely detailed and easy to follow. At first, it was hard to know what classes did what but after using it on a few projects I was amazed at how quickly I could create a working prototype of a design. The time I saved enabled me to complete more projects in less time and make more money in the process.

The more I used Bootstrap, the more I felt like it could be a global standard because it removes a lot of routine tasks when building responsive sites.

Bootstrap was created by Mark Otto and Jacob Thornton[6] at Twitter as a framework to encourage consistency across internal tools. It is now an open source project hosted on GitHub[7] and has seen rapid growth and global use in web applications and websites.

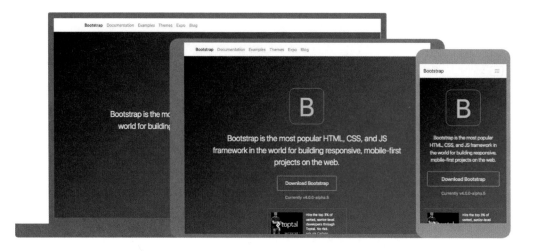

---

6 https://v4-alpha.getbootstrap.com/about/history/
7 https://github.com/twbs/bootstrap

Bootstrap CSS Framework History

- Before 2011   An internal Twitter tool
- August 2011   Released as open source
- January 2012   Bootstrap 2
- August 2013   Bootstrap 3
- August 2015   Bootstrap 4 Alpha
- August 2017   Bootstrap 4 Beta
- January 2018   Bootstrap 4

A Toolkit Built in Style Guide Form

When Bootstrap was first created at Twitter it was built as a toolkit of reusable components with additional documentation and code snippets on how to use them. This helped a team of multiple developers work on a project and have a cohesive methodology on how to build layouts. The documentation and ease of implementation, made it easy to share and reference with others, regardless of their skill level.

So, **the initial intent of Bootstrap was to be a living style guide documentation for a team of developers** to code in the same way following a set of pre-defined rules and components.

Today, Bootstrap Can Be Used in Two Main Ways:

1. Linking to a precompiled version via CDN or locally

2. Linking to a customized build using the Sass source files

On the next page (Fig. 5) I explore the pros and cons of each method and also break them into smaller sub-methods to help you decide which is best for your project.

A System of Components

At this point, you might be wondering what is a component and why does Bootstrap use them? Well, one definition I found was, "A component is a minimal software item that can be tested in isolation." The keyword in that phrase is **isolation**.

Since CSS cascades down to child elements, how do you isolate things and write styles to target specific components and leave everything as is? The solution Bootstrap presented is the use of prefix class naming and sub-classes for variations.

Fig. 4: The International Space Station is made up of isolated components that perform a specific purpose. Combined they create a system of linked components.

Mark Otto wrote on his blog[8], "Each class name begins with a prefix. Class name prefixing makes our code more durable and easier to maintain, but it also better enables us to **scope styles to only the relevant elements.**"

---

8   http://markdotto.com/2012/03/02/stop-the-cascade/

Is Bootstrap Even Necessary?

If you are an experienced web designer or developer you are probably wondering what the benefits are using Bootstrap in your project. Prior to using Bootstrap, I used a boilerplate I wrote myself that consisted of a reset, basic grid, typography, utilities, and media queries. Below are the benefits I have experienced from now using Bootstrap for my projects.

Helps You Save Time

I admit I was the worst at documenting my own work. I would use my boilerplate on a project and then want to make an update to it a month later. But by then, I totally forgot my naming convention. So I would have to spend time reading my code to try to understand what I did. If I couldn't figure it out, I would add new code and leave the old code alone to prevent breaking something. Yup, sound the code bloat alarm.

Bootstrap has amazing documentation on each component. So if I want to update a project I worked on a few months ago that uses Bootstrap I know where to go to find documentation if I get stuck. Also, the more I use Bootstrap the more it is burned into my brain and the less time is spent searching the documentation.

Helps You Avoid Cross-browser Bugs

Prior to using Bootstrap I would get the dreaded emails from clients saying their website they just paid me for doesn't look good on X device. And of course, it is a device I do not currently own or have access to. After hours or searching on Google you finally find a fix on Stack Overflow. You find comfort knowing it is a common problem with Android devices and not something you caused.

Being an open source project, anyone can submit browser bugs and code fixes for it. This is an extremely valuable asset to a developer because you gain confidence knowing your code has been improved by a community to address common browser bugs. No matter how good you are, there is no way you can be aware of every browser inconsistency and the fix necessary. Using Bootstrap, you're standing on the shoulders of giants.

Fig. 5 - The Different Ways to Use Bootstrap

	Method	Use Cases
1a	**Link to CDN Minified** Difficulty: beginner	• Cases where custom branding is not a priority • Backend layouts • Prototypes
1b	**Link to CDN Minified + Custom Stylesheet** Difficulty: beginner	• The method used in this book • Production sites that require unique branding
1c	**Link to CDN Minified + Custom Stylesheet from Sass Files** Difficulty: intermediate	• Production sites that require unique branding
2a	**Link to Custom Build** Difficulty: advanced	• Production sites that require unique branding
2b	**Link to Custom Build + Docs Build** Difficulty: advanced	• Production sites that require unique branding • Multiple developers work on a single project

Pros	Cons
• Fast • Easy to setup • No preprocessor needed	• Lacks unique visual style • Some code bloat of unused components
• Fast • Easy to setup • No preprocessor needed	• The time to inspect and overwrite Bootstrap styles • Some code bloat of unused components
• Some setup time • You gain the benefits of Sass with mixins, variables, and multiple files.	• The time to inspect and overwrite Bootstrap styles • Some code bloat of unused components • Requires knowledge of Sass and compiling
• More setup time • Gain the benefits of Sass • Removes code bloat	• Knowledge of Sass and compiling
• More setup time • Gain the benefits of Sass • Removes code bloat • Create updated documentation	• Knowledge of Sass and compiling • Knowledge of Jekyll and compiling • Documentation updates

Helps You Follow Best Practices

I studied graphic design in college and self-taught myself HTML & CSS from books, YouTube, and blog posts. This mixture of knowledge worked to some degree but I know there are a lot of knowledge gaps. I hit my lack of understanding head-on when I first learned Bootstrap with all of the new terminology written for software engineers.

Bootstrap is not just a framework but a methodology of best practices for front-end design.

Gather a room full of the smartest web designers and developers and let them discuss at length what they think is the best way to write CSS and to organize a project. The result being a distilled version of best practices agreed upon by a large collection of your peers.

Helps You Avoid jQuery Plugin Soup

I know some JavaScript but writing a full-fledged plugin is out of my reach. So I often collected various jQuery plugins into a project to achieve the look and functionality I was looking for.

But I often ran into the following problems:

3. Plugins would not work across browsers
4. Plugin CSS styles would conflict with other CSS styles
5. Plugins would be dependent on different versions of jQuery

Bootstrap contains a collection of jQuery components that you know are stable on modern browsers compatible and works with your jQuery version. Also, the styling matches all of the other components in the your project.

Helps You Be More Marketable

Bootstrap has 73% of the design framework market share[9] as of May 2017. This popularity correlates to the demand for people to know the framework to either update existing systems and or create new ones.

So this will make you more marketable to prospective employers. Indeed.com, a popular job search engine, shows Bootstrap has a lot of job postings compared to other CSS frameworks.

Framework Name	Total Sites
Bootstrap CSS (update to v4?)	12,559,226
HTML5 Boilerplate	4,219,959
960 Grid System	437,120
Unsemantic	74,386
Semantic UI	10,803

Source: BuiltWith as of May, 2017[10]

---

9   https://trends.builtwith.com/docinfo/design-framework
10 https://trends.builtwith.com/docinfo/design-framework

Summary

When your time is billable, every minute you shave off will greatly improve your bottom line. Plus it makes development more fun because you are not declaring redundant CSS properties.

I hope I have shown you how Bootstrap can save you time and make you a better developer in the process. In addition, you will be following industry best practices vetted by an open source community.

Now that you know the history and benefits of using Bootstrap let's dive into what's new in version 4.

Recorded Training Video

Want to learn more about responsive web design and the mobile-first workflow? Watch a 45 minute training video at https://bootstrapcreative.com/b4recording

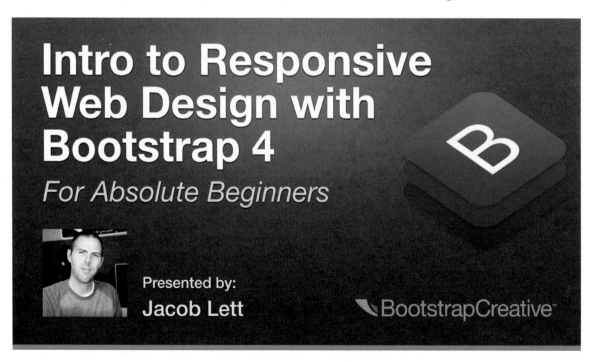

Intro to Responsive Web Design with Bootstrap 4

For Absolute Beginners

Presented by:
Jacob Lett

BootstrapCreative™

What's New in Bootstrap 4

Flexbox Grid

The most important element of any CSS framework is the grid system. The Bootstrap grid has been used on many websites worldwide which make it extremely stable.

This cross-browser support is why you probably are considering using Bootstrap for your website (it was for me). In this section, I will provide an overview of the grid and provide examples to help you quickly apply it to your projects.

Important! Before you begin a project, you should know what set of web browsers you are going to support. This will actually determine what version of Bootstrap you use because Bootstrap 4 is not supported on IE9 and below.

What Versions of IE Do You Need to Support?

So how do you know what browsers to support? If you are redesigning an existing site, I suggest looking at your Google Analytics to see what browser the majority of your site visitors use. Look for trends to determine if it makes sense to remove support for an older browser.

If you have no analytics to work with I suggest looking at StatCounter[1] to see the top browsers in your country. But from my experience, it is best to have a clear understanding of your ideal site visitor. Because there are a lot of factors, tools like StatCounter do not factor in. One of those being corporate environments that are slow to upgrade to newer browsers.

---

1   http://gs.statcounter.com/#desktop-browser_version-ww-monthly-201608-201610-map

One way to get a clear picture of your target site visitor is through surveys or live interviews. Talk to likely site visitors and ask them what browsers they use and if there are any IT restrictions preventing them to upgrade browsers.

Once you have your data and some assumptions follow the decision chart below to determine what Bootstrap version you should use.

Bootstrap Version Decision Chart

I need to support IE10+	Use Bootstrap 4
I need to support IE9+	Use Bootstrap 3
I need to support IE8+	

What is Flexbox?

In Bootstrap 3 and for the majority of websites, the only way to build multi-column layouts was to set column widths and use floats. Then on mobile, you would just remove the float and width property so that it would change to be one column.

Now with flexbox, or flexible box, you will be able to build complex grid layouts with more control and flexibility to adapt the layout as the viewport changes.

If you are familiar with an UL and LI relationship, flexbox is very similar in how it has sub items or flexbox items inside a parent wrapping container. But since flexbox is a display property it can be applied to any parent and child HTML elements and does not have its own HTML element like `<flexbox>`.

Fig. 8 demonstrates[2] how a flexbox grid adjusts the height of sibling columns while a float grid does not. With flexbox, all of your grid columns will share an equal height and you will not have to worry about clearing floated columns.

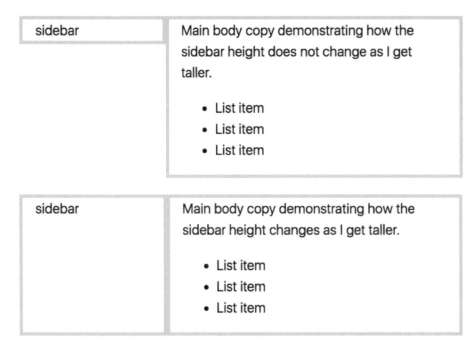

Fig. 8: A two column grid using floats vs. a grid using flexbox

Another exciting feature of flexbox is how it handles vertical alignment[3]. Before flexbox, you had to use various CSS tricks in order to make things align properly. Often having to use more HTML markup than truly necessary. Fig. 9 demonstrates how you can vertically align columns inside a flexbox container with a single CSS property. Bootstrap uses this CSS3 functionality in it's grid class system.

---

2   http://codepen.io/JacobLett/pen/mWGNOz
3   http://codepen.io/JacobLett/pen/vxVVQE

Fig. 9: Flexbox makes vertical alignment easy!

Keep in mind, Bootstrap is a CSS framework that builds upon the core language of CSS. So flexbox is the core CSS technology that Bootstrap uses for grid layout and is not a component created by Bootstrap. So it is helpful to know the fundamentals of flexbox in case you need to override something.

Additional Sources to Learn How Flexbox Works

Take Command of CSS Flexbox[4]

This tutorial compares flexbox to an Army commander to explain how the parent containers control it's child elements. Find this on page #.

Bootstrap 4 flexbox cheat sheet[5]

This printable cross-reference lists all of the Bootstrap flexbox utility classes alongside the native CSS flexbox properties.

Solved by Flexbox[6]

A great summary of common layout challenges flexbox helps to make a lot easier.

---

4   Page #
5   https://bootstrapcreative.com/resources/flexbox-cheat-sheet/
6   https://philipwalton.github.io/solved-by-flexbox/

12 Column Grid

So now that you understand flexbox and why it's superior to floats for layout, lets look at how Bootstrap uses this for their grid system.

The Bootstrap grid system is based on a 12 column grid because the number 12 is divisible by 12, 6, 4, 3, 2. So your column sizes inside each row will need to add up to equal 12. This math makes the grid more flexible for a wide range of layouts.

Common Grid Layout Examples:

- **2 column grid**
  .col-sm-6 + .col-sm-6 = 12

- **2 column golden ratio grid**
  .col-sm-8 + .col-sm-4 = 12

- **3 column grid**
  .col-sm-4 + .col-sm-4 + .col-sm-4 = 12

1	2	3	4	5	6	7	8	9	10	11	12	13	14	15

Fig. 10: By default, Flexbox item widths are equally distributed to fill the width of the container. If you set the column class to `.col` *it makes each column horizontal at all breakpoints. So it doesn't respect the 12 column grid like you think it would as shown in this example.*

1	2	3	4	5	6	7	8	9	10	11	12
13	14	15									

Fig. 11: In this example, I changed the column class to `.col-sm-1` *instead of* `.col` *which restricts the column width even after it has been wrapped. Columns widths are equally distributed to fill the width of the container. Since Bootstrap uses a 12 column grid, it breaks after 12 and the remaining columns are equally distributed.*

The Bootstrap Grid System Has Three Main Parts: C.R.C.

When working with the Bootstrap 12 column grid you have to keep in mind the order of elements and that there are always three parts: a Container, a Row, and any number of Columns.

 Tip: You can remember CRC by thinking of a **C**abin, a **R**oom inside the cabin, and finally **C**hairs inside the room.

If you want all of your page content to be constrained to a max-width, you would just need one `.container` on your entire page. Or if you would like your columns to fill the entire window and have no max-width use `.container-fluid`. Then use a series of row blocks with column divs to build your grid. If your design has no horizontal color banding you could set `.container` to the body tag. However, there is a design trend to have horizontal background colors with the content set to a max-width.

Design is improvement. Design is improvement.

A short paragraph that is contained to a max width by a container. A short paragraph that is contained to a max width by a container. A short paragraph that is contained to a max width by a container. A short paragraph that is contained to a max width by a container. A short paragraph that is contained to a max width by a container. A short paragraph that is contained to a max width by a container.

Form follows function. Form follows function.

The way I achieve this effect[7] is using a section tag with a background color set to it.

`section.bg-primary > .container > .row > .col-sm-6`

---

7   https://bootstrapcreative.com/pattern/row-background-color-full-width/

If you are familiar with a HTML table structure the grid system is very similar.

For example:

```
           table > tr > td
               is like
.container > .row > .col-sm-6
```

Container

`.container` or `.container-fluid`

This is the parent container that determines if the columns should be full-width or not.

Row

`.row`

A horizontal wrapping container for the series of columns it contains.

Columns

`.col` or `.col-*`

A column is a vertical division similar to a table cell. This is where your content goes and has built-in margin to the left and right to prevent text and images from touching each other.

Columns also have grid tiers which tell the columns how they should look at different breakpoints. For example, `.col-sm-6` essentially says, "When the browser window is 576px or higher make this column span 6 of the 12 columns. For anything below 576px make it full width." So when you declare a grid tier you are telling the web browser, make it this size for the **specified breakpoint and all sizes above it**.

Fig. 12: **Bootstrap Grid Tiers and Breakpoints**

xs	**Extra small** <576px	portrait mobile
sm	**Small** ≥576px	landscape mobile
md	**Medium** ≥768px	portrait tablets *navbar collapse*
lg	**Large** ≥992px	landscape tablets
xl	**Extra large** ≥1200px	laptops, desktops, TVs

Conclusion

The Bootstrap CSS Grid System is extremely customizable and helps you to be more efficient in building page layouts. And now with flexbox instead of floats, you will have more control on how your columns are positioned on the page.

Key points

- Uses a 12 column grid and the number of columns has to equal 12
- **C.R.C.** – `.container > .row > .col-*-*`
- Most projects will just need one .container unless you want to do colored row banding
- Setting a grid tier like `.col-sm-6` says for sm and up
- Columns have horizontal padding to create the gutters between individual columns, however, you can remove the margin from rows and padding from columns with `.no-gutters` on the `.row`.
- Grid columns without a set width will automatically layout with equal widths.

View documentation: https://getbootstrap.com/docs/4.0/layout/grid/

Cards

A new component introduced in Bootstrap 4 are cards. Cards replace panels, thumbnails, and wells used in Bootstrap 3.

Card title

Some quick example text to build on the card title and make up the bulk of the card's content.

Go somewhere

A card is essentially a contained chunk of content with a border and inner padding.

You can easily customize the content to fit your needs for endless design combinations. You can add image caps to cards like shown to the right. Cards default to 100% width so its best to add them inside a grid structure so they are responsive. You will also need to add `.img-fluid` to your image so that it scales down.

To demonstrate the range of possibilities, below is an example of tabs being added inside a card for multiple content sections inside a card. View this code demo[8] for more card design possibilities.

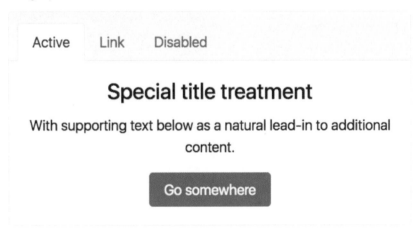

---

8   https://codepen.io/JacobLett/pen/oZmWdd

Card Layout Options

Bootstrap 4 also includes three wrapper classes to change the layout of multiple cards. All you would need to do is create div with one of the classes listed below and place all of your cards inside it. These classes use flexbox to change the layout. Let's now explore the differences between them.

Card Groups - No Gutters

.card-img-top	.card-img-top	.card-img-top	.card-img-top
.card-title	**.card-title**	**.card-title**	**.card-title**
.card-text	.card-text	.card-text	.card-text
.card footer	.card footer	.card footer	.card footer

When you add the wrapper class .card-group it applies flexbox CSS styles to adjust the layout. So the default flexbox characteristics apply: items equally distribute horizontally, and heights of each card match. I could see this class used for a pricing tier chart or any information you want to show has a close relationship.

One issue I encountered with a five card layout is how it looked on tablet breakpoints. See how the last card expands full width in the picture to the right?[9] This lack of uniform sizing doesn't really look good. So I would suggest using a grid structure and adding your cards inside the grid,.

---

9   https://codepen.io/JacobLett/pen/PpVjwo

If you scroll to the bottom of this example[10] you will see how I created the same layout using a grid with the `.no-gutters` class on the row to squeeze everything together. This will give you more control of the layout at different breakpoints.

Card Decks - Gutters

Card decks are similar to card groups but they include gutters, or margin between each card. You use the `.card-deck` wrapper class to create one. These work well on desktop but when you scale down to mobile cards expand full width which lacks uniform sizing.

Similar to card groups, if you scroll to the bottom of this example[11] you will see how I created the same layout using a grid. This strategy will give you more control of how things look at different breakpoints.

Note: Card groups, decks, and columns require some custom styling to add margin below each card.

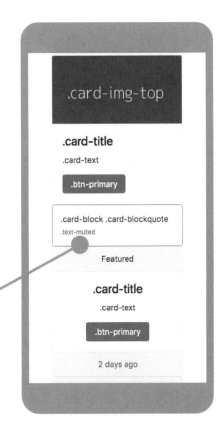

---

10 https://codepen.io/JacobLett/pen/PpVjwo
11 https://codepen.io/JacobLett/pen/QpYgbK

Card Columns - Masonry

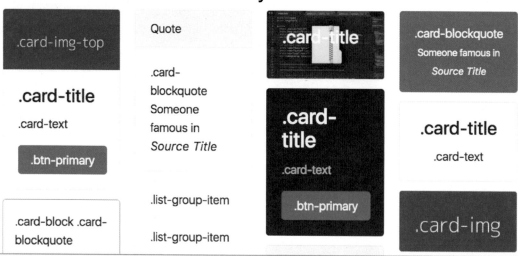

When you add the wrapper class `.card-columns` it applies flexbox CSS styles to adjust the layout. So it changes the flexbox items to flow in columns instead of row. And then does uses column-count[12]: CSS property to change the number of columns in the grid. You can see how this layout works by viewing this demo[13]. I also show various demos of card designs you can create.

The downside of this approach is items are not listed in chronological order. So if you want to list blog posts you may want to look at masonry.js[14].

---

12 https://www.w3schools.com/cssref/playit.asp?filename=playcss_column-count
13 https://codepen.io/JacobLett/pen/oZmWdd
14 http://masonry.desandro.com/

Conclusion

Cards provide a lot of design flexibility and help you create a visual hierarchy[15] in your layout. The card layout classes utilize flexbox to change the layout of the cards but have some issues when you scale down to mobile. For more control, I suggest thinking of cards as content and add them into a grid structure. This will let you control layout at each breakpoint.

Key points

- A card is essentially a contained chunk of content with a border and inner padding.
- If you used Bootstrap 3, cards replace panels, thumbnails, and wells.
- Card groups, cards, and columns have some responsive quirks that may deter from their use. I recommend using a grid structure instead.
- Images inside card groups, cards, and columns require a set width otherwise the images will stretch.

View documentation: https://getbootstrap.com/docs/4.2/components/card/

---

15 https://en.wikipedia.org/wiki/Visual_hierarchy

Spacing Utility Classes

Bootstrap is based on reusable components which have base styles, sub item styles, and design variation styles. But what if you want to change the padding on a jumbotron used on your contact us page?

You could write a page-specific style targeting that jumbotron to add the different padding. Or another way would be to use a new spacing utility like the `.p-lg-5` class.

You are probably thinking, "How is this different from writing an inline style with the padding? Isn't the whole point of CSS to separate styles from markup?" It is essentially a hybrid approach that gives you more flexibility and keeps your styling consistent.

Reasons Why These Classes Help

- Eliminates writing similar and repetitive styles for different pages. Spacing as a reusable utility.

- Prevents overlooking a padding style that should match another page but since they are declared at a page level its gets lost. Having uniform padding/margin utilities help keep things consistent because if you make a change it applies everywhere the class is used.

- The classes are responsive giving you full control on when the padding/margin is applied.

So now you know their benefits, let's look at how to use them.

How They Work

You have probably seen this colored box in Chrome's Developer Tools before. It represents the CSS box model and how padding, border, and margin are applied to a HTML element (shown in blue below).

Color Key:

Content   Padding   Border   Margin

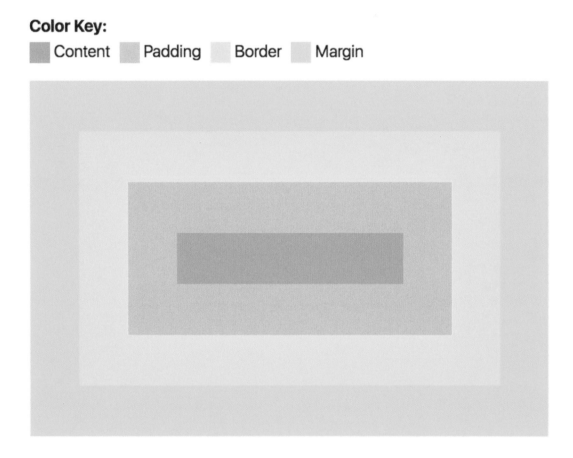

View spacing classes code demo[16]

---

16 http://codepen.io/JacobLett/pen/XMQamB

For xs and up

Since Bootstrap is a mobile first framework, to target spacing on mobile you do not need to specify a breakpoint value like xs in the class.

```
{property}{sides}-{size}
```

For all other breakpoints

For any size above xs you need to add a breakpoint (sm, md, lg, xl). When you do, they apply from that breakpoint up.

```
{property}{sides}-{breakpoint}-{size}
```

Property

Use a lowercase p for padding and a lowercase m for margin. Figure 12 shows examples of both set for all breakpoints xs and up.

Sides

To specify a particular side or sides add the corresponding letter for the side you wish to target.

t	r	b	l	x	y
top	right	bottom	left	left right	top bottom

Breakpoint

If you want your spacing to apply everywhere you can omit a breakpoint. Otherwise, select the breakpoint you would like to apply your spacing. Keep in mind, the spacing is applied to the breakpoint and everything above it. So if you want the spacing to apply to only one breakpoint you will need to use a combination of classes to stop the higher breakpoints from inheriting.

none	sm	md	lg	xl
<576px	≥576px	≥768px	≥992px	≥1200px

To do this use a combination of classes like:

```
class="p-0 p-md-4 p-lg-0"
```

So in this example, I set all breakpoints padding to 0, then specified a padding of 4 on the **md** breakpoint, but I have to stop the padding from flowing to **lg** and **xl** so I add `p-lg-0`.

Size

The values for each level of spacing are a calculation of the base font size which is 16px or 1rem. Below are the pixel equivalents for each numeric spacing value.

0	1	2	3	4	5
0px	4px	8px	16px	24px	48px

View documentation[17]

View spacing classes code demo[18]

---

17 https://getbootstrap.com/docs/4.0/utilities/spacing/
18 http://codepen.io/JacobLett/pen/XMQamB

How It's Different from Bootstrap 3

Bootstrap 4 is a major rewrite of version 3. A lot of classes have been added, renamed, or dropped which will make migration a challenge. The list below is a shortened version of the major updates I think are most important. To read all of the changes, reference their migration page[19].

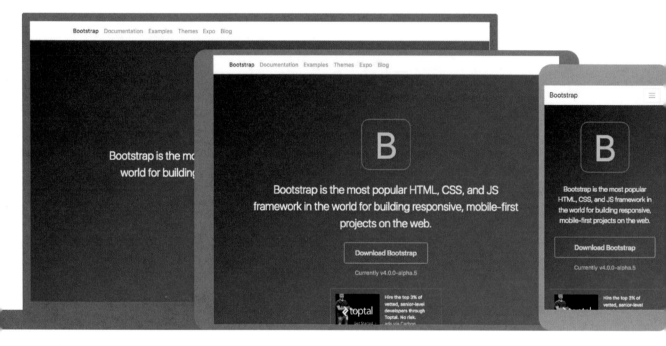

No Longer Supported

- IE8, IE9, and iOS 6 support
- Non-responsive usage of Bootstrap

---

19 https://getbootstrap.com/docs/4.0/migration/

New in Bootstrap 4

- Flexbox is enabled by default with a decreased reliance on floats.
- **Switched from px to rem as it's primary CSS unit,** though pixels are still used for media queries and grid behavior as viewports are not affected by type size.
- Global font-size increased from 14px to 16px.
- Added a new xs grid tier for smaller devices at 576px and below.
- You can now specify when the navbar should collapse using `.navbar-toggleable-{breakpoint}`
- The addition of explicit classes on descendants to make components less dependent on certain HTML elements. For example, `.breadcrumb-item`, is now required on the descendants of `.breadcrumbs` and `.list-inline` now requires that its children list items have the new `.list-inline-item` class applied to them.
- Made display utilities responsive - `.d-none` and `.d-{sm,md,lg,xl}-none`
- Added responsive spacing utilities for padding and margin
- Responsive floats and text alignment

Renamed

- `.img-responsive` to `.img-fluid`
- `.img-rounded` to `.rounded`
- `.img-circle` to `.rounded-circle`
- `.btn-default` to `.btn-secondary`
- `.center-block` to `.mx-auto`
- `.navbar-toggle` is now `.navbar-toggler`
- `.label` to `.tag` so its not confused with a form label tag
- Updated responsive utilities: The `.hidden-*-up` classes hide the element when the viewport is at the given breakpoint or larger. The `.hidden-*-down` classes hide the element when the viewport is at the given breakpoint or smaller

Dropped

- Glyphicons font. FontAwesome is a good alternative. You can use my FontAwesome reference to help you migrate

- The Affix jQuery plugin.

- `.page-header`

- `.btn-xs` class because `.btn-sm` is much smaller

- `.badge` component as it was nearly identical to labels/tags.

Official Bootstrap 4 migration page

https://getbootstrap.com/docs/4.0/migration/

The Design Process

Vision Test

Before we start using Bootstrap, I want you to be familiar with the design process. This four phase process has milestones that require approval by a decision maker before moving onto the next phase. These approvals help to eliminate costly re-work at later stages, delayed projects, and stress.

For example, changing a navigation item name in the design phase could break the layout and require time to re-write styles to accommodate.

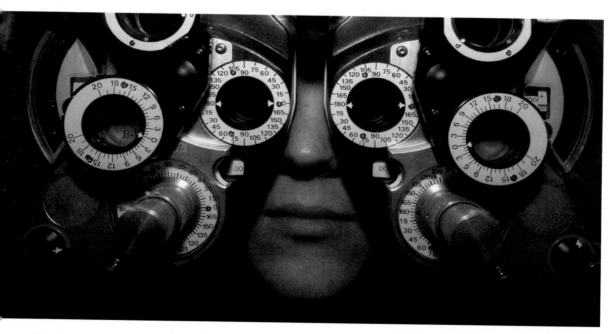

The last time I was at the eye doctor I was fitted for glasses. As I was looking through one of these, my doctor flipped lenses and asked me questions like "Can you see better with these lenses? How about now? Better or worse?" With each lens flip, my vision would get clearer and clearer.

The design process acts in a very similar way in bringing more clarity to the project you are building. Starting out with a blank sheet of paper can be daunting. But by asking a series of questions before you start your design, you can begin to bring clarity to the final solution.

"Research is the gathering of facts. In the absence of facts, you have assumptions. And assumptions are the enemy of design."
— *Mike Monteiro*

The Design Process Phases

The four phases of the design process are Strategy, Prototype, Design, and Delivery. As you progress through the phases you gain more clarity on the final design solution. Each phase requires client sign-off before moving on. These checkpoints or milestones help decrease the chances of late changes causing project delays and increased costs.

Prior to responsive design, layouts could be designed in Photoshop and approved before any code was written. The goal for a developer was to simply "Match the PSD". Today, this is impossible because there are more variables that impact a design than ever before. Smaller screens, slow connection speeds, different web browsers, etc. Today a design requires an iterative process where you achieve a final solution through repeating rounds of analysis and tests.

Instead of first designing pages and templates, you would first focus on designing individual components that are part of a larger design system. You then build your page layouts with these individual components. This enables you to reuse design elements on multiple pages without having to rewrite code.

Starting on a Solid Foundation - Strategy Phase

In this very important phase, you will most likely meet with a client or business manager to determine the goals of the project. In this meeting, you will strive to complete a creative brief which will be an agreed-upon strategy that all success will be measured against. Next, I will describe each section of the creative brief so you can see its importance.

Creative Brief

- **Background** - Why is this project being considered? What is the problem trying to be solved? Increased revenue, smoother process, lead generation, etc.

- **Target audience** - Who are the primary users of the site or application? What needs, wants, and expectations do they have?

- **Goals** - Often the goals will be tied to some measurable outcome like increased revenue, more leads, 10 more positive reviews, etc.

- **Deliverables** - This section lists what you will produce and what the client will expect to receive once the project is completed.

- **Budget** - Makes sure you can provide a solution within a determined budget.

- **Schedule** - This helps to set expectations on when the project will be completed and how the process will work.

- **Brand Guidelines** - Most clients have existing brand guidelines you will need to follow in order for your design to align with other materials they have.

- **Design Strategy** - This will most likely be completed after the meeting by you or your team. This is your solution to achieve the client's goals and describes the work you plan to do before you actually do it. If your solution doesn't work in word form it will never work as a fully coded site.

The Remaining Phases

Once the creative brief has been signed off, you can then branch off this document and begin adding layers of more clarity to your solution. The design phase will mostly like require collaboration between a UX designer and UI designer to develop a clickable prototype and some design variations. This workflow will greatly decrease your chances of unhappy clients and costly rework.

1. Strategy

Interviews and research to define a clear design strategy to achieve a measurable business objectives.

Approvals needed

🗋 Creative Brief

2. Prototype

You will define the site architecture, page naming, and site content to be presented. The client will approve basic functionality.

Approvals needed

🗋 Wireframe & architecture
🗋 Site copy
🗋 Clickable prototype

3. Design

Work through branding and visual style. The client should approve code and not flat Photoshop files.

Approvals needed

🗋 Clickable design of homepage
🗋 Development site

4. Delivery

Publish final site and collect analytics for three months. Report back and review performance.

Approvals needed

🗋 Final signoff
🗋 Analytics report

The Design Phases Used in This Book

In this book, we will be spending our time focusing on the prototype and design phases.

These phases are closely related and could also be broken up into UX and UI. Prototypes focus on identifying content, naming, hierarchy and site architecture. The design phase converts wireframes into final layouts with graphics and branding.

This book will not be able to demonstrate how to generate pencil thumbnail sketches or perform design exploration in a graphics program. Both of these require a deep dive into design theory, branding, and design software. If you would like to learn these skills, please signup on this page[20] to be notified of a future book or training on this subject.

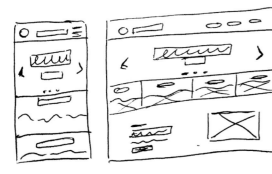
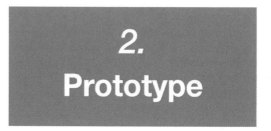

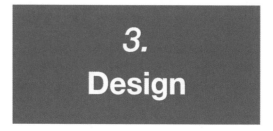

---

20 https://bootstrapcreative.com/shop/web-design-book/

Build a Homepage

Introduction

To help make the projects you build more practical, I am going to use my business name and pretend I am a medium sized web design agency. I am hiring you to help me build a website to help me gain leads online.

On the next page, I provide the creative brief to help you learn about my company and the people I serve. Since I already have a logo and other marketing material I would like to continue using similar colors and fonts for consistency.

If you ever end up freelancing, you will often work with businesses who do not have an existing brand strategy and you will need to help them develop one. This initial project demonstrates your concern for brand consistency and how it helps differentiate them from their competition.

In addition, I provide a completed design strategy outlining the goals and expectations for the homepage design. This strategy is what we used to guide us through developing a wireframe and then a clickable prototype.

Design is the bridge that brings the business strategy to life.

- Geoff Suvalko

Creative Brief

Background

BootstrapCreative would like to attract new business opportunities by demonstrating their expertise and past success with other companies. They do not have a large budget for advertising so the website needs to be optimized for search engines by continually adding blog posts and case studies.

Target audience

BootstrapCreative works with CMO's or CEO's who are looking to grow their business using digital marketing.

Goals

10 new high quality leads a month

Deliverables

Wireframe, clickable prototype, development site, and final site hosted with domain

Budget

$2,000

Schedule

Would like to have completed in 4 weeks because they are attending an industry tradeshow.

Brand Guidelines

Web design services company who helps businesses tell their story online. They obsess over the creative process to ensure efficiency and accuracy in meeting business objectives.

Audience

- Local professional service businesses who depend on a steady stream of leads.
- Businesses who have existing desktop websites and want to redesign to make them responsive.

How They are Unique

Digital craftsmen who believe design needs to tell a story to achieve measurable results.

#0275d8   #292b2c

#636c72   #e2e2e2

Lato Bold
Helvetica Neue Regular
Helvetica Neue Medium
Helvetica Neue Bold

Design Strategy

Design considerations

- Customers are tech savvy and primarily marketing professionals or small business owners

- Marketers who are very data driven and expect a ROI or measurable return on investment

- BootstrapCreative spends a lot of time researching their clients needs and business objectives and champion craftsmanship.

Solution

- Feature a carousel to highlight unique selling points.

- Article headings will clearly demonstrate growth and measurable return on investment.

- Service offerings will be prominent so it is clear what BootstrapCreative provides. The high quality design will demonstrate competency and the ability to achieve quality work.

- Optimized for search engines to attract local search traffic and position BootstrapCreative as an expert in their local community. There will also be a content management system so you can add blog posts, events, and case studies to attract organic search traffic.

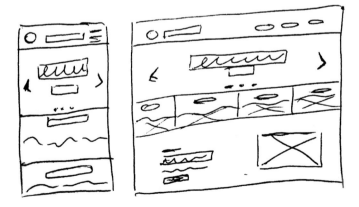

Wireframe

Wireframing is the most important step of any design. It forces you to think about how things will be organized and function.

What content is really needed? What behaviors would someone want to perform on this page? What will they look for the most? Once we have a vision of what we want to build the next step is to explore the existing Bootstrap components to see what we can re-use in our project.

Visual Hierarchy and Naming

When designing a page layout it is important to consider the hierarchy. What are the goals of the page and how can you make those goals easier to achieve? Your design can use size, color, position, and proximity to define a hierarchy of information on a page. You can learn more about this design principle in my article[1].

Tools

Wireframing tools: Balsamiq[2], Moqups[3], PowerPoint[4], Inkscape[5], and Google Slides[6]. Site architecture tools: Coggle[7] and MindNode[8].

---

1   https://bootstrapcreative.com/what-is-visual-hierarchy/
2   https://balsamiq.com/
3   https://moqups.com/
4   https://products.office.com/en-us/powerpoint
5   https://inkscape.org/en/
6   https://docs.google.com/presentation/u/0/
7   https://coggle.it/
8   https://mindnode.com/

Fixed-top Navbar
Carousel
Services
Case Study (text:image)
Testimonial
Case Study (image:text)
Blog Posts
Services
Footer

Build Prototype

Now that we have a wireframe, the next step is to select existing Bootstrap components that we can use in our project.

Browse Bootstrap's documentation or if you purchased the Complete package, the *Components Visual Reference* is a handy tool to quickly review components.

Make notes of components that need further customization and those that need to be written from scratch. This step helps to eliminate code duplication and saves time in re-using existing components in your project.

Bootstrap Components Used in This Layout

A. Navbar

B. Carousel

C. Cards

D. Buttons

E. Navs

F. Forms

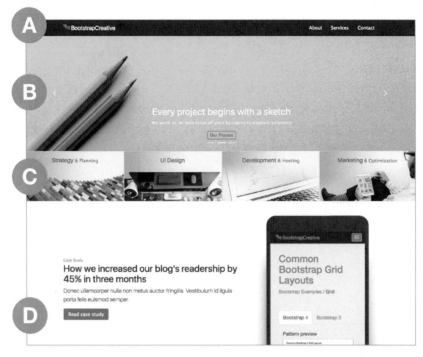

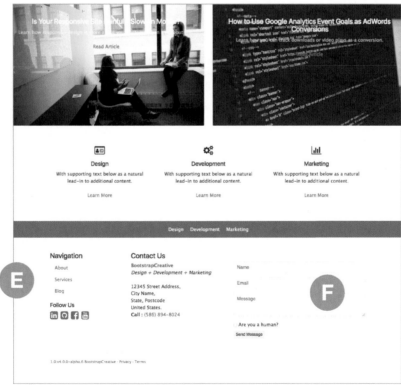

Step 1

Download the starter project .zip which contains the folder structure, images, and blank files. Save and unzip the folder where you would like to keep your website projects. I personally use XAMPP to run a local server and generally save all of my web projects in my **htdocs** folder that way I can test my projects at localhost/project-name. If you have never setup a local server before, you can follow my tutorial[9] to learn the steps.

Project File and Folder Structure

🗁 **homepage-prototype**
    🗁 **css**
        🗋 homepage.css
    🗁 **img**
    🗋 index.html
    🗁 **js**
        🗋 homepage.js
        🗋 defer.js
        🗁 **vendor**
            🗋 jquery-3.1.1.min.js

Download the starter project files
https://bootstrapcreative.com/b4hp01

Want to download the finished project files to check your work?

Learn more about the *Bootstrap 4 Toolkit*
https://bootstrapcreative.com/b4toolkit

9   https://bootstrapcreative.com/xampp

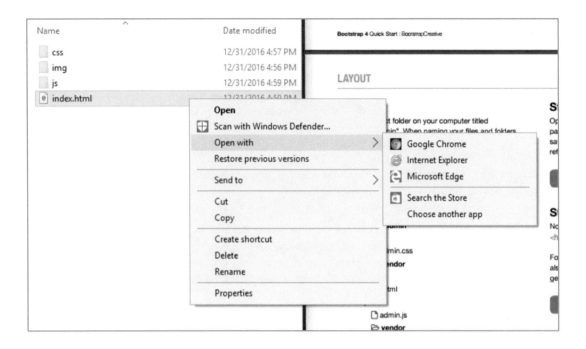

Windows - If this is your first time using Sublime Text you will also need to right click the files with extensions .html, .css, .js and hover over **OPEN WITH** *and click* **CHOOSE ANOTHER APP** *to then choose Sublime Text. This will make sure these files open in your text editor.*

Step 2

Open `index.html` in your text editor. Now copy and paste the page boilerplate code into `index.html` and save. This is a basic HTML page template without any reference to Bootstrap or outside scripts.

Copy this code
https://bootstrapcreative.com/b4hp02

```
<!DOCTYPE html>
<html lang="en">
<head>
    <meta charset="utf-8">
    <meta http-equiv="X-UA-Compatible" content="IE=edge">
    <meta name="viewport" content="width=device-width, initial-scale=1,
shrink-to-fit=no">
    <!-- The above 3 meta tags *must* come first in the head; any other head
content must come *after* these tags -->
    <title>BootstrapCreative | Design + Development + Marketing</title>
    <meta name="description" content="">
    <meta name="author" content="">
    <!-- Favicons - http://realfavicongenerator.net/ -->
    <link rel="apple-touch-icon" sizes="180x180" href="img/favicons/apple-
touch-icon.png">
    <link rel="icon" type="image/png" href="img/favicons/favicon-32x32.png"
sizes="32x32">
    <link rel="icon" type="image/png" href="img/favicons/favicon-16x16.png"
sizes="16x16">
    <link rel="manifest" href="img/favicons/manifest.json">
    <link rel="mask-icon" href="img/favicons/safari-pinned-tab.svg"
color="#5bbad5">
    <meta name="theme-color" content="#ffffff">
    <!-- Open Graph and Schema if needed goes below this line - https://
webcode.tools/open-graph-generator/business -->
    <!--
    ##################################################
    C S S - bootstrap, custom styles
    ##################################################
    -->
</head>
<body>
    <!--
    ##################################################
    N A V B A R
    ##################################################
    -->
    <!--
    ##################################################
    C A R O U S E L
    ##################################################
    -->
```

```
<h1>Hello world!</h1>
<!--
##################################################
I M A G E   C A R D S
##################################################
-->
<!--
##################################################
C A S E S T U D Y 1
##################################################
-->
<!--
##################################################
Q U O T E
##################################################
-->
<!--
##################################################
C A S E S T U D Y 2
##################################################
-->
<!--
##################################################
B L O G   P O S T S
##################################################
-->
<!--
##################################################
S E R V I C E S
##################################################
-->
<!--
##################################################
B R A N D   M E S S A G E
##################################################
-->
<!--
##################################################
F O O T E R
##################################################
-->
```

```
    <!--
    ################################################
    J A V A S C R I P T - jquery, bootstrap, plugins
    Placed at the end of the document so the pages load faster
    ################################################
    -->
</body>
</html>
```

Step 3

Copy the minified Bootstrap CSS code and paste above the closing </head> tag.

Copy this code
https://bootstrapcreative.com/b4hp03

```
<!--
######################################################
C S S - bootstrap, custom styles
######################################################
-->
<!-- Bootstrap core CSS -->
<link rel="stylesheet" href="https://stackpath.bootstrapcdn.com/
bootstrap/4.2.1/css/bootstrap.min.css" integrity="sha384-GJzZqFGwb1QTTN6wy59f
fF1BuGJpLSa9DkKMp0DgiMDm4iYMj70gZWKYbI706tWS" crossorigin="anonymous">

<!-- FontAwesome Icons -->
<link rel="stylesheet" href="https://use.fontawesome.com/releases/v5.6.3/css/
all.css" integrity="sha384-UHRtZLI+pbxtHCWp1t77Bi1L4ZtiqrqD80Kn4Z8NTSRyMA2Fd3
3n5dQ8lWUE00s/" crossorigin="anonymous">

<!-- Lato Display Font from Google Fonts -->
<link href="https://fonts.googleapis.com/css?family=Lato:400,400i,700,700i"
rel="stylesheet">

<!-- Custom styles for this template -->
<link href="css/homepage.css" rel="stylesheet">
```

Step 4

Next, copy the minified Bootstrap JavaScript code and paste it above the closing `</body>` tag.

This code snippet contains Bootstrap scripts and its dependencies, which are `jQuery` and `tether.js` (which is used for tooltips).

What's a code dependency? In other words, Bootstrap requires other code to work properly and so depends on additional libraries created by another developer. Dependencies have to be referenced/loaded before Bootstrap can run.

Copy this code
https://bootstrapcreative.com/b4hp04

```
<!--
###################################################
J A V A S C R I P T - jquery, bootstrap, plugins
Placed at the end of the document so the pages load faster
###################################################
-->
<!-- jQuery - Grab from a CDN and if not available grab a local copy -->
<script src="https://code.jquery.com/jquery-3.3.1.slim.min.js"
integrity="sha384-q8i/X+965Dz00rT7abK41JStQIAqVgRVzpbzo5smXKp4YfRvH+8abtTE1Pi
6jizo" crossorigin="anonymous"></script>
<!-- local fallback in case the CDN is down -->
<script>
  window.jQuery || document.write('<script src="js/vendor/jquery-3.3.1.min.
js"><\/script>')
</script>

<!-- Bootstrap core JS -->
```

```
<script src="https://cdnjs.cloudflare.com/ajax/libs/popper.js/1.14.6/
umd/popper.min.js" integrity="sha384-wHAiFfRlMFy6i5SRaxvfOCifBUQy1xHdJ/
yoi7FRNXMRBu5WHdZYu1hA6ZOblgut" crossorigin="anonymous"></script>
<script src="https://stackpath.bootstrapcdn.com/bootstrap/4.2.1/js/bootstrap.
min.js" integrity="sha384-B0UglyR+jN6CkvvICOB2joaf5I4l3gm9GU6Hc1og6Ls7i6U/
mkkaduKaBhlAXv9k" crossorigin="anonymous"></script>

<!-- Custom Javascript -->
<script src="js/homepage.js"></script>

<!-- Defer scripts that are not critical to the initial page load. -->
<script type="text/javascript">
  function downloadJSAtOnload() {
  var element = document.createElement("script");
  // Your scripts would go inside this defer.js
  // Use case would be "enhancements" like animations, share buttons, etc.
  element.src = "js/defer.js";
  document.body.appendChild(element);
  }
  if (window.addEventListener)
  window.addEventListener("load", downloadJSAtOnload, false);
  else if (window.attachEvent)
  window.attachEvent("onload", downloadJSAtOnload);
  else window.onload = downloadJSAtOnload;
</script>

<!-- Google Analytics code goes here if needed -->
```

This snippet also includes a script tag with some JavaScript code inside. This code loads a JS file `defer.js` after the entire page is finished loading. This helps increase page load time by removing the non-critical code from the initial page load. Things like Disqus comment scripts, social widgets, and enhancements like animations.

Then open your `index.html` file inside your browser by dragging and dropping it onto a blank browser tab window. You are now able to navigate your project files, edit them, and see the results in your browser window.

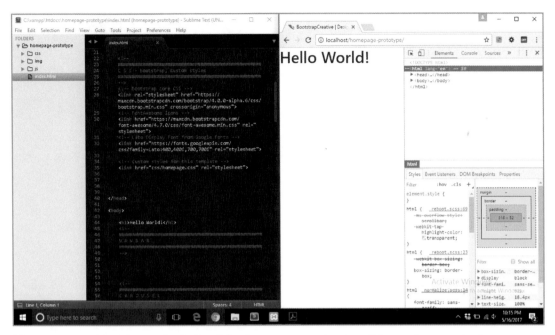

Your screen should now look like this. I recommend using this workspace to force yourself to view your design mobile first.

Step 5

For our homepage layout, we want some content to be fluid width and some content to be constrained to the breakpoints. To achieve this we will be using the `.container` class on a per section basis instead of having all of our body content inside of it.

Example: `nav > .container`

Next, copy and paste the navbar code to add it below the opening `<body>` tag.

Copy this code
https://bootstrapcreative.com/b4hp05

```
<!--
##################################################
N A V B A R
##################################################
-->
<!-- If you need sticky-top to work in lower versions of IE https://github.
com/filamentgroup/fixed-sticky -->
<nav class="navbar navbar-expand-md navbar-dark bg-dark sticky-top">
    <!-- One of the primary actions on mobile is to call a business - This
displays a phone button on mobile only -->

    <div class="navbar-toggler-right">
        <button class="navbar-toggler" type="button" data-toggle="collapse"
data-target="#navbar" aria-controls="navbarTogglerDemo02" aria-
expanded="false" aria-label="Toggle navigation">
            <span class="navbar-toggler-icon"></span>
        </button>
    </div>

    <a class="navbar-brand" href="#">
        <img src="img/bootstrapcreative-icon.svg" width="25" height="25"
class="d-inline-block align-top" alt="">
        <span class="">BootstrapCreative </span>
    </a>

    <div class="collapse navbar-collapse" id="navbar">
        <nav class="nav d-flex flex-column flex-md-row w-100 justify-content-
end">
            <a class="flex-fill text-center text-light nav-link"
href="#about">About</a>
            <a class="flex-fill text-center text-light nav-link"
href="#services">Services</a>
            <a class="flex-fill text-center text-light nav-link"
href="#contact">Contact</a>
        </nav>
    </div>
</nav>
```

Step 6

Next, copy the carousel code and paste to replace the carousel comment section and replace this line of code `<h1>Hello World!</h1>`.

Copy this code
https://bootstrapcreative.com/b4hp06

```
<!--
#################################################
C A R O U S E L
#################################################
-->
<div id="carousel" class="carousel slide carousel-fade" data-ride="carousel"
data-interval="6000">
    <ol class="carousel-indicators">
        <li data-target="#carousel" data-slide-to="0" class="active"></li>
        <li data-target="#carousel" data-slide-to="1"></li>
        <li data-target="#carousel" data-slide-to="2"></li>
    </ol>
    <div class="carousel-inner" role="listbox">
        <div class="carousel-item active">
            <a href="">
                <!--
                If you need more browser support use https://scottjehl.github.
io/picturefill/
                If a picture looks blurry on a retina device you can add a
high resolution like this
                <source srcset="img/blog-post-1000x600-2.jpg, blog-post-
1000x600-2@2x.jpg 2x" media="(min-width: 768px)">

                What image sizes should you use? This can help - https://
codepen.io/JacobLett/pen/NjramL
                -->
                <picture>
                  <source srcset="img/carousel-2000x400-1.jpg" media="(min-
width: 1400px)">
                  <source srcset="img/carousel-1400x400-1.jpg" media="(min-
width: 768px)">
```

```
                    <source srcset="img/carousel-800x400-1.jpg" media="(min-
width: 576px)">
                    <img srcset="img/carousel-600x400-1.jpg" alt="responsive
image" class="d-block img-fluid">
            </picture>

            <div class="carousel-caption">
                <div>
                    <h2>Digital Craftsmanship</h2>
                    <p>We meticously build each site to get results</p>
                    <span class="btn btn-sm btn-outline-secondary">Learn
More</span>
                </div>
            </div>
        </a>
    </div>
    <!-- /.carousel-item -->
    <div class="carousel-item">
        <a href="">
            <!--
            If you need more browser support use https://scottjehl.github.
io/picturefill/
            If a picture looks blurry on a retina device you can add a
high resolution like this
            <source srcset="img/blog-post-1000x600-2.jpg, blog-post-
1000x600-2@2x.jpg 2x" media="(min-width: 768px)">

            What image sizes should you use? This can help - https://
codepen.io/JacobLett/pen/NjramL
            -->
            <picture>
                <source srcset="img/carousel-2000x400-2.jpg" media="(min-
width: 1400px)">
                <source srcset="img/carousel-1400x400-2.jpg" media="(min-
width: 768px)">
                <source srcset="img/carousel-800x400-2.jpg" media="(min-
width: 576px)">
                <img srcset="img/carousel-600x400-2.jpg" alt="responsive
image" class="d-block img-fluid">
            </picture>

            <div class="carousel-caption justify-content-center align-
items-center">
```

```
                    <div>
                        <h2>Every project begins with a sketch</h2>
                        <p>We work as an extension of your business to explore
solutions</p>
                        <span class="btn btn-sm btn-outline-primary">Our
Process</span>
                    </div>
                </div>
            </a>
        </div>
        <!-- /.carousel-item -->
        <div class="carousel-item">
            <a href="">
                <!--
                If you need more browser support use https://scottjehl.github.
io/picturefill/
                If a picture looks blurry on a retina device you can add a
high resolution like this
                <source srcset="img/blog-post-1000x600-2.jpg, blog-post-
1000x600-2@2x.jpg 2x" media="(min-width: 768px)">

                What image sizes should you use? This can help - https://
codepen.io/JacobLett/pen/NjramL
                -->
                <picture>
                    <source srcset="img/carousel-2000x400-3.jpg" media="(min-
width: 1400px)">
                    <source srcset="img/carousel-1400x400-3.jpg" media="(min-
width: 768px)">
                    <source srcset="img/carousel-800x400-3.jpg" media="(min-
width: 576px)">
                    <img srcset="img/carousel-600x400-3.jpg" alt="responsive
image" class="d-block img-fluid">
                </picture>

                <div class="carousel-caption justify-content-center align-
items-center">
                    <div>
                        <h2>Performance Optimization</h2>
                        <p>We monitor and optimize your site's long-term
performance</p>
                        <span class="btn btn-sm btn-secondary">Learn How</
span>
```

```
                </div>
            </div>
        </a>
    </div>
    <!-- /.carousel-item -->
    </div>
    <!-- /.carousel-inner -->
    <a class="carousel-control-prev" href="#carousel" role="button" data-
slide="prev">
        <span class="carousel-control-prev-icon" aria-hidden="true"></span>
        <span class="sr-only">Previous</span>
    </a>
    <a class="carousel-control-next" href="#carousel" role="button" data-
slide="next">
        <span class="carousel-control-next-icon" aria-hidden="true"></span>
        <span class="sr-only">Next</span>
    </a>
</div>
<!-- /.carousel -->
```

Step 7

Next, copy the image cards code and paste it to replace the image cards comment section.

Copy this code
https://bootstrapcreative.com/b4hp07

```
<!--
#################################################
I M A G E   C A R D S
#################################################
-->
<section id="image-cards" class="">
    <div class="container-fluid marketing px-0">
        <!-- Three columns of text below the carousel -->
        <div class="row no-gutters">
```

```
                <div class="col-lg-3 col-sm-6 ">
                    <div class="card bg-light">
                        <a href="">
                            <img class="card-img img-fluid" src="img/image-cards-
600x300-4.jpg" alt="Card image">
                            <div class="card-img-overlay text-center">
                                <h5 class="card-title">Strategy <small>&
Planning</small></h5>
                            </div>
                        </a>
                    </div>
                </div>
                <!-- /.col-lg-4 -->
                <div class="col-lg-3 col-sm-6">
                    <div class="card bg-light">
                        <a href="">
                            <img class="card-img img-fluid" src="img/image-cards-
600x300-1.jpg" alt="Card image">
                            <div class="card-img-overlay text-center">
                                <h5 class="card-title">UI Design</h5>
                            </div>
                        </a>
                    </div>
                </div>
                <!-- /.col-lg-4 -->
                <div class="col-lg-3  col-sm-6">
                    <div class="card bg-light">
                        <a href="">
                            <img class="card-img img-fluid" src="img/image-cards-
600x300-2.jpg" alt="Card image">
                            <div class="card-img-overlay text-center">
                                <h5 class="card-title">Development <small>&
Hosting</small></h5>
                            </div>
                        </a>
                    </div>
                </div>
                <!-- /.col-lg-4 -->
                <div class="col-lg-3 col-sm-6">
                    <div class="card bg-light">
                        <a href="">
                            <img class="card-img img-fluid" src="img/image-cards-
```

```
600x300-3.jpg" alt="Card image">
                        <div class="card-img-overlay text-center">
                            <h5 class="card-title">Marketing <small>&
Optimization</small></h5>
                        </div>
                    </a>
                </div>
            </div>
            <!-- /.col-lg-4 -->
        </div>
        <!-- /.row -->
    </div>
    <!-- /.container -->
</section>
<!-- /#marketing-tiles  -->
```

Step 8

Next, copy the case study code and paste to replace the case study 1 comment section.

Copy this code
https://bootstrapcreative.com/b4hp08

```
<!--
###################################################
C A S E   S T U D Y 1
###################################################
-->
<section id="case-study-1" class="my-5">
    <div class="container">
        <div class="row align-items-center">
            <div class="col-md-7 py-5">
                <small>Case Study</small>
                <h2>How we increased our blog's readership by 45% in three
months</h2>
                <p class="lead">Donec ullamcorper nulla non metus auctor
fringilla. Vestibulum id ligula porta felis euismod semper.</p>
```

```
                <a href="" class="btn btn-primary btn-md">Read case study</a>
            </div>
            <!-- /.col-md-7 -->
            <div class="col-md-5 align-self-end">
                <img class="img-fluid mx-auto img-border-b" src="img/mobile-
screenshot.png" alt="First slide">
            </div>
            <!-- /.col-md-5 -->
        </div>
    </div>
</section>
<!-- #case-study-1 -->
```

Step 9

Next, copy the quote code and paste to replace the quote comment section.

Copy this code
https://bootstrapcreative.com/b4hp09

```
<!--
####################################################
Q U O T E
####################################################
-->
  <section id="quote" class="bg-parallax py-5 mt-3">
      <div class="container">
          <blockquote class="blockquote py-5 text-center border-0">
              <p class="mb-0 display-4">It's much easier to double your
business by doubling your conversion rate than by doubling your traffic.</p>
              <footer class="blockquote-footer ">Jeff Eisenberg</footer>
          </blockquote>
      </div>
      <!-- /.container -->
  </section>
```

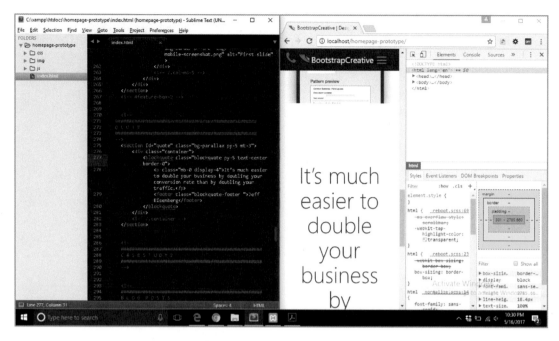

Your screen should now look like this.

Step 10

Next, copy the case study 2 code and paste to replace the case study 2 comment section.

```
<!--
##################################################
C A S E S T U D Y 2
##################################################
-->
<section id="case-study-2" class="my-5">
    <div class="container">
        <div class="row align-items-center">
            <div class="col-md-7 push-md-5 py-5">
```

```
        <small>Case Study</small>
        <h2>Going responsive helped CompanyX grow their organic search
traffic by 45%</h2>
        <p class="lead">Donec ullamcorper nulla non metus auctor
fringilla. Vestibulum id ligula porta felis euismod semper.</p>
        <a href="" class="btn btn-primary btn-md">Read case study</a>
    </div>
    <!-- /.col-md-7 -->
    <div class="col-md-5 pull-md-7 align-self-end">
        <img class="img-fluid mx-auto img-border-b" src="img/mobile-
screenshot.png" alt="First slide">
    </div>
    <!-- /.col-md-5 -->
        </div>
    </div>
</section>
<!-- #case-study-2 -->
```

Step 11

Next, copy the blog posts code and paste to replace the blog posts comment section.

Copy this code
https://bootstrapcreative.com/b4hp11

```
<!--
##################################################
B L O G   P O S T S
##################################################
-->
<section id="blog-posts" class="overflow-h">
  <div class="row">
      <div class="col-md-6 pl-0">
          <div class="card bg-dark text-light overlay overlay-b-3 border-0">
              <!--
              If you need more browser support use https://scottjehl.github.
io/picturefill/
```

```
                If a picture looks blurry on a retina device you can add a high
resolution like this
                <source srcset="img/blog-post-1000x600-2.jpg, blog-post-
1000x600-2@2x.jpg 2x" media="(min-width: 768px)">

                What image sizes should you use? This can help - https://
codepen.io/JacobLett/pen/NjramL
                -->
            <picture>
                <source srcset="img/blog-post-1000x600-1.jpg" media="(min-
width: 768px)">
                <source srcset="img/blog-post-800x400-1.jpg" media="(min-
width: 576px)">
                <img srcset="img/blog-post-800x600-1.jpg" alt="responsive
image" class="card-img img-fluid">
            </picture>
            <div class="card-img-overlay text-center mt-4">
                <h4 class="card-title">Is Your Responsive Site Painfully
Slow on Mobile?</h4>
                <div class="card-text">
                    <p>Learn how responsive design is more about your
customer than it is about you.</p>
                    <ul class="nav justify-content-center">
                        <li class="nav-item">
                            <a class="nav-link active" href="#">Read
Article</a>
                        </li>
                    </ul>
                </div>
            </div>
        </div>
        <!-- /.card -->
    </div>
    <!-- /.col-sm-6 -->
    <div class="col-md-6 pr-0 pt-2 pt-md-0">
        <div class="card bg-dark text-light overlay overlay-b-3 border-0">
            <!--
            If you need more browser support use https://scottjehl.github.
io/picturefill/
            If a picture looks blurry on a retina device you can add a high
resolution like this
            <source srcset="img/blog-post-1000x600-2.jpg, blog-post-
1000x600-2@2x.jpg 2x" media="(min-width: 768px)">
```

```
            What image sizes should you use? This can help - https://
codepen.io/JacobLett/pen/NjramL
                -->
            <picture>
                <source srcset="img/blog-post-1000x600-2.jpg" media="(min-
width: 768px)">
                <source srcset="img/blog-post-800x400-2.jpg" media="(min-
width: 576px)">
                <img srcset="img/blog-post-800x600-2.jpg" alt="responsive
image" class="card-img img-fluid">
            </picture>

            <div class="card-img-overlay text-center mt-4">
                <h4 class="card-title">How to Use Google Analytics Event
Goals as AdWords Conversions</h4>
                <div class="card-text">
                    <p>Learn how you can track downloads or video plays as
a conversion.</p>
                    <ul class="nav justify-content-center">
                        <li class="nav-item">
                            <a class="nav-link active" href="#">Read
Article</a>
                        </li>
                    </ul>
                </div>
            </div>
        </div>
        <!-- /.card -->
    </div>
    <!-- /.col-sm-6 -->
  </div>
</section>
```

Step 12

Next, copy the services code and paste to replace the services comment section.

```
<!--
################################################
S E R V I C E S
################################################
-->
<section id="services" class="my-5">
    <div class="container">
        <div class="row">
            <div class="col-md-4">
                <div class="card text-center border-0 bg-none">
                    <div class="card-body">
                        <p>
                            <i class="fa fa-id-card-o fa-2x" aria-
hidden="true"></i>
                        </p>
                        <h5 class="card-title">Design</h5>
                        <p class="card-text">With supporting text below as a
natural lead-in to additional content.</p>
                        <ul class="nav justify-content-center">
                            <li class="nav-item">
                                <a class="nav-link" href="#">Learn More</a>
                            </li>
                        </ul>
                    </div>
                </div>
                <!-- /.card -->
            </div>
            <!-- /.col-md-4 -->
            <div class="col-md-4">
                <div class="card text-center border-0 bg-none">
                    <div class="card-body">
```

```
                        <p>
                            <i class="fa fa-cogs fa-2x" aria-hidden="true"></
i>
                        </p>
                        <h5 class="card-title">Development</h5>
                        <p class="card-text">With supporting text below as a
natural lead-in to additional content.</p>
                        <ul class="nav justify-content-center">
                            <li class="nav-item">
                                <a class="nav-link" href="#">Learn More</a>
                            </li>
                        </ul>
                    </div>
                </div>
                <!-- /.card -->
            </div>
            <!-- /.col-md-4 -->
            <div class="col-md-4">
                <div class="card text-center border-0 bg-none">
                    <div class="card-body">
                        <p>
                            <i class="fa fa-bar-chart fa-2x" aria-
hidden="true"></i>
                        </p>
                        <h5 class="card-title">Marketing</h5>
                        <p class="card-text">With supporting text below as a
natural lead-in to additional content.</p>
                        <ul class="nav justify-content-center">
                            <li class="nav-item">
                                <a class="nav-link" href="#">Learn More</a>
                            </li>
                        </ul>
                    </div>
                </div>
                <!-- /.card -->
            </div>
            <!-- /.col-md-4 -->
        </div>
        <!-- /.row -->
    </div>
    <!-- /.container -->
</section>
```

Step 13

Next, copy the brand message code and paste to replace the brand message comment section.

Copy this code
https://bootstrapcreative.com/b4hp13

```
<!--
##################################################
B R A N D   M E S S A G E
##################################################
-->
<section id="brand-message" class="bg-primary py-3">
    <div class="container text-light text-center">
      Design <span class="text-light">+</span> Development <span class="text-light">+</span> Marketing
    </div>
    <!-- /.container -->
</section>
```

Step 14 *Final Step*

Next, copy the footer code and paste to replace the footer comment section.

Copy this code
https://bootstrapcreative.com/b4hp14

```
<!--
##################################################
F O O T E R
##################################################
-->
```

```
<footer class="py-5" id="footer">
   <div class="container">
      <div class="row">
         <div class="col-md-3">
            <div class="row">
               <div class="col-sm-6 col-md-12">
                  <h4>Navigation</h4>
                  <nav class="nav d-flex flex-column">
                     <a class="nav-link" href="#">About</a>
                     <a class="nav-link" href="#">Services</a>
                     <a class="nav-link" href="#">Blog</a>
                  </nav>
               </div>
               <div class="col-sm-6 col-md-12">
                  <h5 class="mt-3 mt-sm-0 mt-md-3">Follow Us</h5>
                  <!-- https://bootstrapcreative.com/pattern/custom-
social-media-share-buttons/ -->
                  <div class="social">
                     <a href="https://www.linkedin.com/in/jacoblett"
id="share-li" class="sharer button"><i class="fab fa-2x fa-linkedin pr-1"></
i></a>
                     <a href="https://github.com/JacobLett" id="share-
gh" class="sharer button"><i class="fab fa-2x fa-github-square pr-1"></i></a>
                     <a href="https://www.facebook.com/
bootstrapcreative/" id="share-fb" class="sharer button"><i class="fab fa-2x
fa-facebook-square pr-1"></i></a>
                     <a href="https://twitter.com/BootstrapC" id="share-
tw" class="sharer button"><i class="fab fa-2x fa-youtube-square pr-1"></i></a>
                  </div>
               </div>
            </div>
         </div>
         <!-- .col-sm-6 -->
         <div class="col-md-9">
            <h4 class="mt-4 mt-md-0" id="contact">Contact Us</h4>
            <div class="row">
               <div class="col-sm-5">
                  <!--
                  Generate your local business schema own
                  https://supple.com.au/tools/local-business-schema-
generator/
```

```
                         -->
                    <div itemscope itemtype="http://schema.org/
LocalBusiness">
                        <a itemprop="url" href="https://bootstrapcreative.
com/">
                            <div itemprop="name"><strong>BootstrapCreati
ve</strong></div>
                        </a>
                        <div itemprop="description"><em>Design +
Development + Marketing</em></div>
                        <br>
                        <div itemprop="address" itemscope itemtype="http://
schema.org/PostalAddress">
                            <span itemprop="streetAddress">12345 Street
Address</span>,
                            <br>
                            <span itemprop="addressLocality">City Name</
span>,
                            <br>
                            <span itemprop="addressRegion">State</span>,
<span itemprop="postalCode">Postcode</span>
                            <br>
                            <span itemprop="addressCountry">United States</
span>.
                            <br>
                        </div>
                        <strong>Call : </strong><span
itemprop="telephone"><a href="tel:1-586-894-8024">(586) 894-8024</a></span>
                        <br>
                    </div>
                </div>
                <div class="col-md-7">
                    <form class="mt-4 mt-md-0">
                        <div class="form-group">
                            <label for="formGroupExampleInput" class="sr-
only">Name</label>
                            <input type="text" class="form-control bg-
faded-4" id="name" placeholder="Name">
                        </div>
                        <div class="form-group">
                            <label for="formGroupExampleInput" class="sr-
only">Email</label>
                            <input class="form-control bg-faded-4"
```

```
type="email" value="" id="email" placeholder="Email">
                        </div>
                        <div class="form-group">
                            <label for="formGroupExampleInput" class="sr-
only">Message</label>
                            <textarea class="form-control bg-faded-4"
id="message" rows="3" placeholder="Message"></textarea>
                        </div>
                        <div class="custom-control custom-checkbox">
                            <input type="checkbox" class="custom-control-
input" id="spam">
                            <label class="custom-control-label"
for="spam">Are you a human?</label>
                        </div>
                        <button type="submit" class="btn btn-secondary
btn-sm mt-2">Send Message</button>
                    </form>
                </div>
            </div>
            <!-- .col-sm-6 -->
        </div>
    </div>
    <p class="mt-5">
        <hr class="bg-faded-3">
        <small class="text-light">
        © BootstrapCreative · <a href="#" class="text-light">Privacy</a> ·
<a href="#" class="text-light">Terms</a>
        </small>
    </p>
    </div><!-- .container -->
</footer>
```

Summary

Great job. You now have a working homepage using Bootstrap 4. We used Bootstrap's default styles to get a working prototype to quickly demonstrate functionality. The prototype gets the basic idea down but it needs some refinements.

In the next section, we will write some custom CSS styles and add some scripts to make everything look the way we want. See you there.

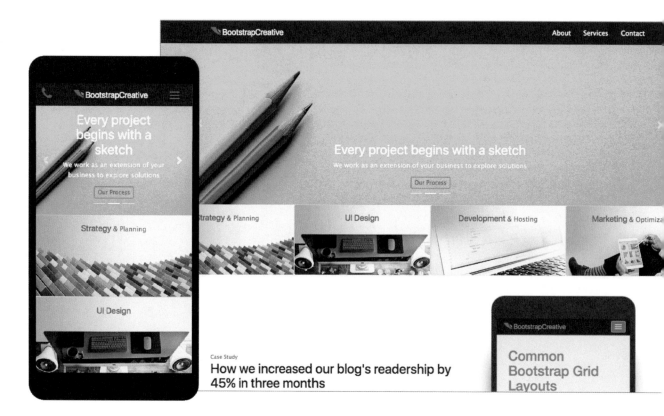

Customize the Design

Where to Start

If we refer back to the design process on page 30, we are now in the design phase. In this phase, we will explore design options and then begin to build a polished design that we can use for testing and approval.

Design Exploration - Fast Forward

Now that you have an approved wireframe, architecture, and page content you can begin exploring different visual solutions. Every designer has their own method but I recommend sketching with paper and pencil first.

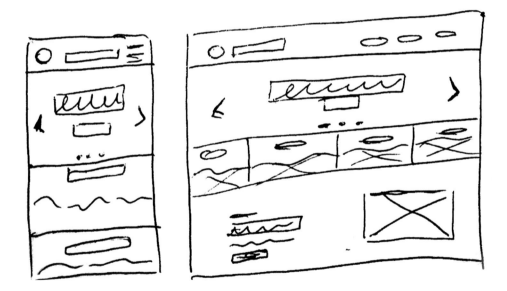

It is easier to flush out multiple ideas on paper than it is to draw shapes in a design program. Also, if it doesn't work as a sketch it will never work as a final design.

Once you have a sketch you like you can then move to a design program like Photoshop, Adobe XD, or Sketch. These apps will help you work out aesthetics, colors, typography, spacing, and graphics before writing any code. Some designers skip this step and go right to code and design in the browser. I personally think this limits your creativity especially if you use Bootstrap. **The UI of Bootstrap should not influence your design**. Following this progression will greatly reduce the chances of your site looking too much like a Bootstrap site.

Since design is such a broad topic and would require a lot of explanation I am going to skip past this process and move right to development. If you would like to learn these skills, please signup on this page[10] to be notified of a future book or training on this subject.

Clickable Design

Before responsive design, it was much easier to convert a desktop design and convert it to code because everything was fixed width and not much would change.

Today, we have to design for different breakpoints, devices, and bandwidths. Each with their own set of nuances and challenges. Because of this, I recommend never showing a client a flat Photoshop design. Ok, let's look at how we are going to improve the design.

It is not enough that we build products that function. We also need to build products that bring joy and excitement, pleasure and fun, and, yes, beauty to people's lives.

—— Don Norman

10 https://bootstrapcreative.com/shop/web-design-book/

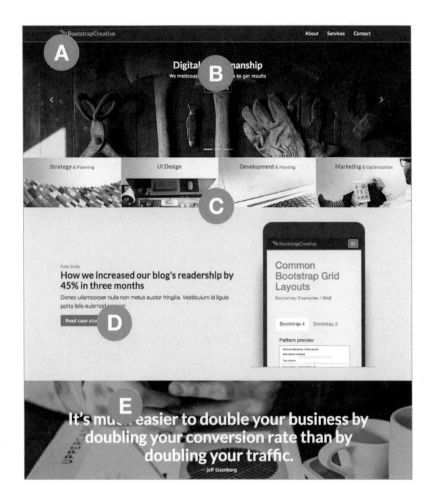

A. Navbar Branding

Add blue border to the bottom and change link color

B. Carousel Captions

Move the captions to the top

C. Image Cards

Adjust image widths

D. Vertical Centered Content

Make the text vertically centered with the image

E. Parallax Background Image

Set a background image that is fixed on scroll

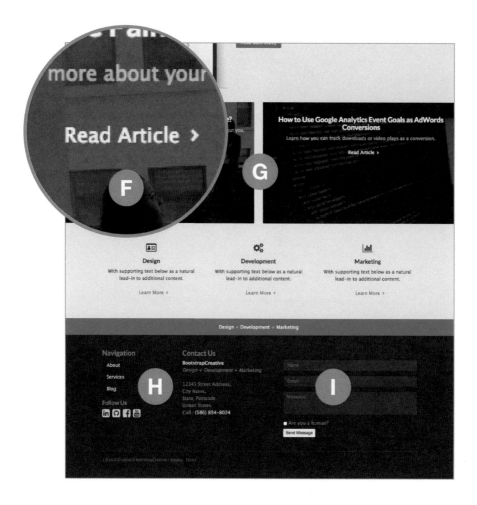

F. Add Right Arrow to Nav Links

Add arrow with CSS and not HTML

G. Text Overlay on Image Cards

Add a black overlay on top of the image
to improve text readability

H. Nested Columns

Add columns with breakpoints that
make sense

I. Muted Form Inputs

The form inputs have too much contrast
and are hard on the eyes

Step 1

In order to override the default Bootstrap styles, we have to reference our own CSS and JS files placed **after the Bootstrap files**. The browser loads the page from the top down, so our styles override what the browser was told to do by Bootstrap because they are listed after it.

Open homepage.css in your text editor.

At the top of the stylesheet, I added some common reference information there like rem to pixels, breakpoints, and brand colors. I also have three main sections: Grid & Type, Utilities, and Components. If you purchased the Pro package, the *Web Design Primer* mentions organizing your CSS styles by component instead of by page. This helps to keep styles organized and prevents styles getting missed if a change is made to the base styles.

First, copy some global styles to change the body background color and set some typography styles. Paste them below the grid and type comment section.

Copy this code
https://bootstrapcreative.com/b4hd01

```
/*
################################################
G R I D  &  T Y P E
################################################
*/

body {
  background: #e2e2e2;
}

/* Set a display font for headings and quotes */
h1, h2, h3, h4, h5,
.navbar-brand, blockquote p,
.display-1, .display-2, .display-3, .display-4 {
```

```
    font-family: 'Lato', sans-serif;
    font-weight: 700;
}

section {
    overflow: hidden;
}

.blockquote-footer {margin-top:0.5rem;}

#footer {
    background-color: #292b2c;
    color: #808080;
}

#footer a,
#footer a:hover,
#footer a:active {
    color: #ccc;
}

#footer .nav-link:hover {
    text-decoration: underline;
}

footer .form-control {
    border:none;
}
```

Step 2

Next, copy the background utility styles and paste them below the background utilities comment section.

Copy this code
https://bootstrapcreative.com/b4hd02

```
/*
:::::::::::::::::::::::::::::::::::::::::::::::::::::::
Background utilities
*/
.bg-parallax {
  background-repeat: no-repeat;
  background-position: center center;
  -webkit-background-size: cover;
  -moz-background-size: cover;
  -o-background-size: cover;
  background-size: cover;
  background-attachment: fixed;
}

/* cards have a white background by default and this class helps you make
them transparent */
.bg-none {
  background-color: transparent;
}
.text-light a {color:#fff!important;}
.bg-faded-1 {
  background-color: #c5c8c9;
}
.bg-faded-1 {
  background-color: #c5c8c9;
}
.bg-faded-2 {
  background-color: #93989a;
}
.bg-faded-3 {
  background-color: #585d5f;
}
.bg-faded-4 {
  background-color: #3c3f40;
}
.bg-faded-5 {
  background-color: #292b2c;
}
```

Step 3

Next, copy the image border styles and paste them below the image border comment section.

Copy this code
https://bootstrapcreative.com/b4hd03

```
/*
::::::::::::::::::::::::::::::::::::::::::::::::::::::::::
Image Border
Applies a light gray border based on class
all, top, right, bottom, left
*/
.img-border {
  border: 1px solid #808080;
}

.img-border-t {
  border-top: 1px solid #808080;
}

.img-border-r {
  border-right: 1px solid #808080;
}

.img-border-b {
  border-bottom: 1px solid #808080;
}

.img-border-l {
  border-left: 1px solid #808080;
}
```

Step 4

Next, copy the overlay background styles and paste them below the overlay background comment section.

Copy this code
https://bootstrapcreative.com/b4hd04

```css
/*
::::::::::::::::::::::::::::::::::::::::::::::::::::::::
Overlay Background Color
Helps darken or lighten image that has text on top
*/
.overlay,
.overlay {
  position: relative;
}

.overlay:before,
.overlay:before {
  content: '';
  position: absolute;
  left: 0;
  top: 0;
  width: 100%;
  height: 100%;
  display: inline-block;
}

.overlay-b-1:before {
  background: rgba(0, 0, 0, 0.2);
}

.overlay-b-2:before {
  background: rgba(0, 0, 0, 0.4);
}

.overlay-b-3:before {
```

```
    background: rgba(0, 0, 0, 0.6);
}

.overlay-b-4:before {
    background: rgba(0, 0, 0, 0.8);
}

.overlay-b-5:before {
    background: rgba(0, 0, 0, 0.9);
}

.overlay-w-1:before {
    background: rgba(255, 255, 255, 0.2);
}

.overlay-w-2:before {
    background: rgba(255, 255, 255, 0.4);
}

.overlay-w-3:before {
    background: rgba(255, 255, 255, 0.6);
}

.overlay-w-4:before {
    background: rgba(255, 255, 255, 0.8);
}

.overlay-w-5:before {
    background: rgba(255, 255, 255, 0.9);
}
```

Step 5

Next, copy the navbar styles and paste below the navbar comment section.

Copy this code
https://bootstrapcreative.com/b4hd05

```
/*
:::::::::::::::::::::::::::::::::::::::::::::::::::::
Navbar
*/
.navbar {
  border-bottom:2px solid #0275d8;
}
.navbar-brand span {
  color: #89969e;
}

#navbar-call i {
  vertical-align: middle;
  line-height: 40px;
}

.fixedsticky {
  top: 0;
}
```

Step 6

Next, copy the carousel styles and paste below the carousel comment section.

Copy this code
https://bootstrapcreative.com/b4hd06

```
/*
::::::::::::::::::::::::::::::::::::::::::::::::::::::
Carousel
*/
.carousel {
  background-color: #191919;
}

.carousel-caption {
  top: 10%;
}

/* The description text interferes with the indicator nav
so this hides on narrow mobile
*/
.carousel-caption p {
  display:none;
}
@media (min-width: 500px) {
  .carousel-caption p {
    display:block;
  }
}

/* centers the carousel image on super wide screens */
.carousel-item img {
  margin:0 auto;
}
```

Step 7

Next, copy the card navigation styles and paste below the card navigation comment section.

```css
/*
:::::::::::::::::::::::::::::::::::::::::::::::::::::::
Card navigation with right angle character
*/

.card .nav-item {
  position: relative;
}

.card .nav-link:hover {
  text-decoration: underline;
}

.card .nav-item:after {
  content: "\f054";
  font-family: FontAwesome;
  font-size: 60%;
  position: absolute;
  top: 0;
  right: 0;
  display: inline-block;
  padding: .5em 0;
  line-height: 2rem;
  color: #0275d8;
}

/* image card with dark backgrounds to have white links */
.card.bg-dark .nav-link,
.card.bg-dark .nav-item:after {
  color: #fff;
```

```
}

/* image card with light backgrounds to have dark links */
.card.bg-light a {
  color: inherit;
}
```

Step 8 *Final Step*

Next, copy the quote styles and paste below the quote comment section.

Copy this code
https://bootstrapcreative.com/b4hd08

```
/*
:::::::::::::::::::::::::::::::::::::::::::::::::::::::
Quote
Change background image tall (800 x 800) to wide (1500 x 800)
dimensions are increased slightly to account for retina displays
*/
#quote {
  background-image: url('../img/quote-800x800.jpg');
}
#quote p {
  font-size: 2.5rem;
}
@media (min-width: 600px) {
  #quote {
    background-image: url('../img/quote-1500x800.jpg');
  }
  #quote p {
    font-size: 3.5rem;
  }
}
```

Summary

Great job. You now have a polished homepage using Bootstrap 4. We pushed our prototype of default Bootstrap components to match our desired design.

In the next section, we will follow the same workflow to build our CMS dashboard for this site.

Get FREE Bootstrap 4 Cheat Sheets

https://bootstrapcreative.com/b4bundle

Build a Dashboard

Introduction

In the previous section we designed and built the homepage. Now we need to build the admin of the content management system.

On the next page, I provide the same creative brief to help you learn about my company and the people I serve. Since I already have a logo and other marketing material I would like to continue using similar colors and fonts for consistency.

If you ever end up freelancing, you will often work with businesses who do not have an existing brand strategy and you will need to help them develop one. This initial project demonstrates your concern for brand consistency and how it helps differentiate them from their competition.

In addition, I provide a completed design strategy outlining the goals and expectations for the admin dashboard design. This strategy is what we used to guide us through developing a wireframe and then a clickable prototype.

If we want users to like our software, we should design it to behave like a likeable person: respectful, generous and helpful.

- Alan Cooper, Software Designer and Programmer

Creative Brief

Background

BootstrapCreative would like to attract new business opportunities by demonstrating their expertise and past success with other companies. They do not have a large budget for advertising so the website needs to be optimized for search engines by continually adding blog posts and case studies.

Target audience

BootstrapCreative works with CMO's or CEO's who are looking to grow their business using digital marketing.

Goals

BootstrapCreative would like to have a CMS admin where they could monitor analytics and quickly add pages, posts, and local training events.

Deliverables

Wireframe, clickable prototype, development site, and final site hosted with domain

Budget

$2,000

Schedule

Would like to have completed in 4 weeks because they are attending an industry tradeshow.

Brand Strategy

Web design services company who helps businesses grow online. They obsess over the creative process to ensure efficiency and accuracy in meeting business objectives.

Audience

- Local professional service businesses who depend on a steady stream of leads.
- Businesses who have existing desktop websites and want to redesign to make them responsive.

How they are unique

Digital craftsmen who believe design needs to tell a story to achieve measurable results.

#0275d8   #292b2c

#636c72   #e2e2e2

Lato Bold
Helvetica Neue Regular
Helvetica Neue Medium
Helvetica Neue Bold

Design Strategy

Design considerations

- Employees would like the ability to add posts on their mobile devices.

- Need three user levels: admin, editor, and author

- Ability to message other employees inside the admin

Solution

- A top navbar will contain notifications and logged in user information.

- A secondary sidebar navigation will be used to navigate between the different content types.

- The dashboard will contain dynamic charts to visually display analytics as well as a summary of recent content added or in draft mode.

Wireframing is the most important step of any design. It forces you to think about how things will be organized and function.

Visual Hierarchy and Naming

When designing a page layout it is important to consider the hierarchy. What are the goals of the page and how can you make those goals easier to achieve? Your design can use size, color, position, and proximity to define a hierarchy of information on a page. You can learn more about this design principle in my article[1].

Tools

Wireframing tools: Balsamiq[2], Moqups[3], PowerPoint[4], Inkscape[5], and Google Slides[6]. Site architecture tools: Coggle[7] and MindNode[8].

What content is really needed? What behaviors would someone want to perform on this page? What will they look for the most? Once we have a vision of what we want to build the next step is to explore the existing Bootstrap components to see what we can re-use in our project.

---

1   https://bootstrapcreative.com/what-is-visual-hierarchy/
2   https://balsamiq.com/
3   https://moqups.com/
4   https://products.office.com/en-us/powerpoint
5   https://inkscape.org/en/
6   https://docs.google.com/presentation/u/0/
7   https://coggle.it/
8   https://mindnode.com/

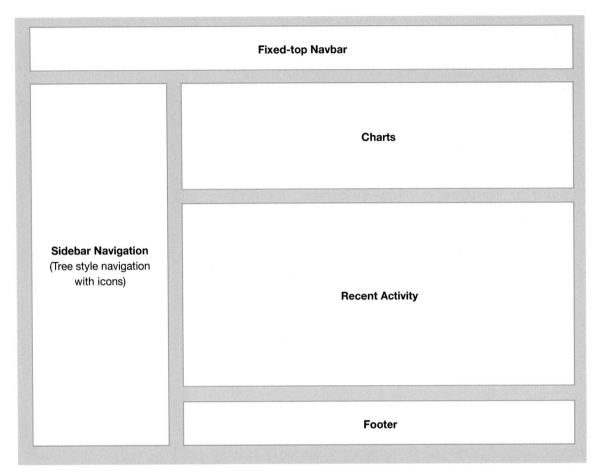

Once you have a vision of what we want to build the next step is to explore the existing Bootstrap components to see what we can re-use in our project.

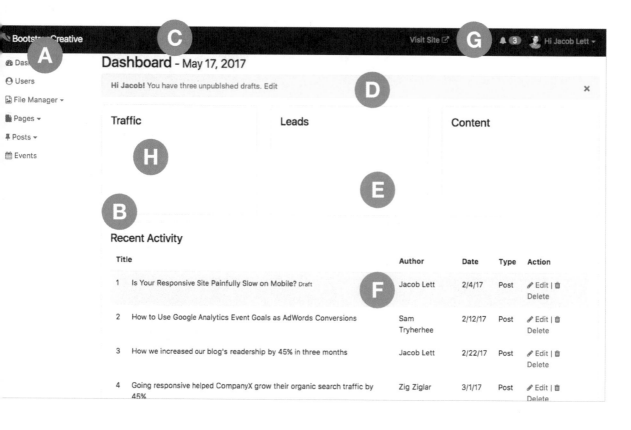

Bootstrap Components Used in This Layout

A. Dropdown

B. Card

C. Navbar

D. Alert

E. Card Deck

F. Table

G. Badge

H. Custom - Will need to find a chart javascript library to display data in charts

Step 1

Download the starter project .zip which contains the folder structure, images, and blank files. Save and unzip the folder where you would like to keep your website projects. I personally use XAMPP to run a local server and generally save all of my web projects in my htdocs folder that way I can test my projects at localhost/project-name. If you have never setup a local server before you can follow my tutorial to learn the steps.

📂 **admin-prototype**
    📂 **css**
        📄 admin.css
    📂 **img**
    📄 index.html
    📂 **js**
        📄 admin.js
        📂 **vendor**
            📄 jquery-3.1.1.min.js

Download the starter project files
https://bootstrapcreative.com/b4ap01

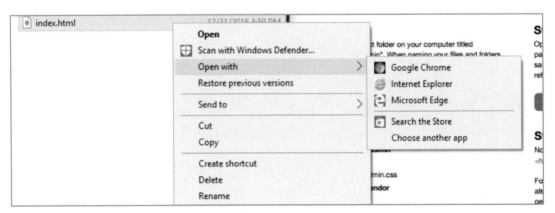

Windows - If this is your first time using Sublime Text you will also need to right click the files with extensions .html, .css, .js and hover over **OPEN WITH** *and click* **CHOOSE ANOTHER APP** *to then choose your text editor. This will make sure these files open in your text editor.*

Step 2

Open `index.html` in your text editor. In the Appendix, I provide instructions on how to setup a mobile-first workspace. Now copy and paste the page boilerplate code into `index.html` and save. This is a basic HTML page template without any reference to Bootstrap our outside scripts.

Copy this code
https://bootstrapcreative.com/b4ap02

```
<!DOCTYPE html>
<html lang="en">
  <head>
    <meta charset="utf-8">
    <meta http-equiv="X-UA-Compatible" content="IE=edge">
    <meta name="viewport" content="width=device-width, initial-scale=1,
shrink-to-fit=no">
    <!-- The above 3 meta tags *must* come first in the head; any other head
content must come *after* these tags -->
    <meta name="description" content="">
    <meta name="author" content="">
    <!-- Favicons - http://realfavicongenerator.net/ -->
    <link rel="apple-touch-icon" sizes="180x180" href="img/favicons/apple-
touch-icon.png">
    <link rel="icon" type="image/png" href="img/favicons/favicon-32x32.png"
sizes="32x32">
    <link rel="icon" type="image/png" href="img/favicons/favicon-16x16.png"
sizes="16x16">
    <link rel="manifest" href="img/favicons/manifest.json">
    <link rel="mask-icon" href="img/favicons/safari-pinned-tab.svg"
color="#5bbad5">
    <meta name="theme-color" content="#ffffff">
    <title>BootstrapCreative Admin</title>
```

```
<!--
######################################################
C S S - bootstrap, custom styles
######################################################
-->

</head>
<body class="admin">
<!--
######################################################
N A V B A R
######################################################
-->

<!--
######################################################
B O D Y
######################################################
-->
<h1>Hello World!</h1>

<!--
######################################################
J A V A S C R I P T - jquery, bootstrap, plugins
Placed at the end of the document so the pages load faster
######################################################
-->

</body>
</html>
```

Step 3

Copy the minified Bootstrap CSS code and paste above the closing </head> tag.

Copy this code
https://bootstrapcreative.com/b4ap03

```
<!--
####################################################
C S S - bootstrap, custom styles
####################################################
-->
<link rel="stylesheet" href="https://stackpath.bootstrapcdn.com/
bootstrap/4.2.1/css/bootstrap.min.css" integrity="sha384-GJzZqFGwb1QTTN6wy59f
fF1BuGJpLSa9DkKMp0DgiMDm4iYMj70gZWKYbI706tWS" crossorigin="anonymous">
<!-- FontAwesome Icons -->
<link rel="stylesheet" href="https://use.fontawesome.com/releases/v5.6.3/css/
all.css" integrity="sha384-UHRtZLI+pbxtHCWp1t77Bi1L4ZtiqrqD80Kn4Z8NTSRyMA2Fd3
3n5dQ8lWUE00s/" crossorigin="anonymous">
```

Step 4

Copy the minified Bootstrap JavaScript code and paste above the closing </body> tag.

This code snippet contains Bootstrap scripts and its dependencies, which are jQuery and tether.js (which is used for tooltips).

What's a dependency? In other words, Bootstrap requires other code to work properly and so depends on additional libraries created by another developer. Dependencies have to be referenced/loaded before Bootstrap can run.

Copy this code
https://bootstrapcreative.com/b4ap04

```
<!--
##################################################
J A V A S C R I P T - jquery, bootstrap, plugins
Placed at the end of the document so the pages load faster
##################################################
-->

<!-- jQuery - Grab from a CDN and if not available grab a local copy -->
<script src="https://code.jquery.com/jquery-3.3.1.slim.min.js"
integrity="sha384-q8i/X+965DzO0rT7abK41JStQIAqVgRVzpbzo5smXKp4YfRvH+8abtTE1Pi
6jizo" crossorigin="anonymous"></script>
<!-- local fallback in case the CDN is down -->
<script>
  window.jQuery || document.write('<script src="js/vendor/jquery-3.3.1.min.
js"><\/script>')
</script>


<!-- Bootstrap core JS -->
<script src="https://cdnjs.cloudflare.com/ajax/libs/popper.js/1.14.6/
umd/popper.min.js" integrity="sha384-wHAiFfRlMFy6i5SRaxvf0CifBUQy1xHdJ/
yoi7FRNXMRBu5WHdZYu1hA6ZOblgut" crossorigin="anonymous"></script>
<script src="https://stackpath.bootstrapcdn.com/bootstrap/4.2.1/js/bootstrap.
min.js" integrity="sha384-B0UglyR+jN6CkvvICOB2joaf5I4l3gm9GU6Hc1og6Ls7i6U/
mkkaduKaBhlAXv9k" crossorigin="anonymous"></script>
```

Step 5

Then open your `index.html` file inside your browser by dragging and dropping it onto a blank browser tab window. You are now able to navigate your project files, edit them, and see the results in your browser window.

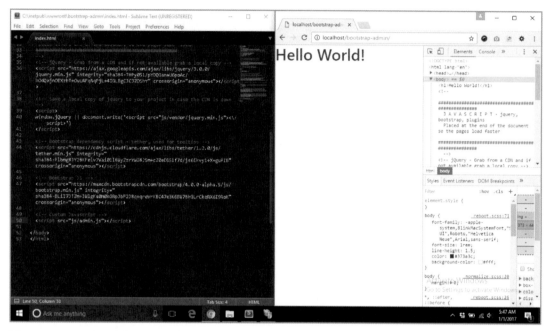

Your screen should now look like this. I recommend using this workspace because it forces you to view your design mobile first.

Step 6

Now let's begin building the layout with the necessary components.

First, copy the code for the Bootstrap grid and paste and replace this line of code `<h1>Hello World!</h1>`.

Copy this code
https://bootstrapcreative.com/b4ap06

```
<!--
###################################################
B O D Y
###################################################
-->
<div class="container-fluid">
  <div class="row">

    <!--
    ###################################################
    S I D E B A R
    ###################################################
    -->
    <div class="col-lg-2 sidebar">

    </div>
    <!-- /.sidebar -->

    <!--
    ###################################################
    M A I N   C O N T E N T
    ###################################################
    -->
    <div class="col main">

    </div>
    <!-- /.main -->
  </div>
  <!-- /.row -->

</div>
<!-- /.container-fluid -->
```

You will notice I added a `.sidebar` class to the narrow column and a `.main` class to the larger column. This helps to identify the main sections of the page and will help us write custom CSS styles later on.

To clearly differentiate between your custom classes and those contained in Bootstrap, you could also prefix your classes with a recognizable string of characters. Like `.bc-main` and `.bc-sidebar` to stand for your brand name in my case BootstrapCreative.

`.container-fluid` is added so that the main content is fluid and expands to the full width of the screen.

Step 7

Next, copy and paste the navbar code to add it below the `<body>` tag and above the `.container-fluid` body section you just added. This will make the navbar and main content independent of each other which will give us more control in a later step.

Copy this code
https://bootstrapcreative.com/b4ap07

```
<!--
##################################################
N A V B A R
##################################################
-->
<!-- If you need sticky-top to work in lower versions of IE https://github.
com/filamentgroup/fixed-sticky -->
<nav class="navbar navbar-expand-sm navbar-dark bg-dark sticky-top ">

  <div class="navbar-toggler-right">
    <button class="navbar-toggler" type="button" data-toggle="collapse" data-
target="#navbar" aria-controls="navbar"
      aria-expanded="false" aria-label="Toggle navigation">
      <span class="navbar-toggler-icon"></span>
    </button>
  </div>
  <!-- Important - make sure to have the toggler button outside of the
```

```
container -->

  <a class="navbar-brand" href="#">
    <img src="img/bootstrapcreative-icon.svg" width="25" height="25" class="d-
inline-block align-top" alt="">
    <span class="">BootstrapCreative </span>
  </a>
  <div class="collapse navbar-collapse" id="navbar">
    <ul class="nav navbar-nav justify-content-end w-100">
      <li class="nav-item">
        <a class="nav-link" href="../../homepage/layout/" target="_
blank">Visit Site <i class="fa fa-external-link"
          aria-hidden="true"></i> </a>
      </li>
      <li class="nav-item">
        <a class="nav-link" href="#">Link</a>
      </li>
      <li class="nav-item">
        <a class="nav-link" href="#">Link</a>
      </li>
      <li class="nav-item float-lg-right">
        <a href="" class="nav-link "><i class="fa fa-bell text-warning" aria-
hidden="true"></i> <span class="badge-pill badge-danger text-light">3</span></
a>
      </li>
      <li class="nav-item dropdown user">

        <a class="nav-link dropdown-toggle" href="#" role="button"
id="responsiveNavbarDropdown" data-toggle="dropdown"
          aria-haspopup="true" aria-expanded="false"><img src="https://secure.
gravatar.com/avatar/38eff4a7ab7f391783f71ccb38508df6?s=30"
          alt="" class="rounded-circle"> Hi Jacob Lett</a>

        <div class="dropdown-menu" aria-labelledby="responsiveNavbarDropdown">
          <a class="dropdown-item" href="#">Edit My Profile</a>
          <a class="dropdown-item" href="#">Log Out</a>
          <a class="dropdown-item" href="#">Help</a>
        </div>
      </li>
    </ul>
  </div>
</nav>
```

Step 8

Next, copy and paste the sidebar navigation and add it inside `.col-lg-2` `.sidebar` div.

Copy this code
https://bootstrapcreative.com/b4ap08

```html
<!-- sidebar navigation -->
<ul class="nav flex-column">
  <li class="nav-item">
    <a class="nav-link active" href="#"><i class="fa fa-tachometer-alt" aria-hidden="true"></i> Dashboard</a>
  </li>
  <li class="nav-item">
    <a class="nav-link" href="#"><i class="fa fa-user-circle" aria-hidden="true"></i> Users</a>
  </li>
  <li class="nav-item dropdown dropdown-tree btn-group">
    <a class="nav-link dropdown-toggle" data-toggle="dropdown" href="#" role="button" aria-haspopup="true" aria-expanded="false"><i class="fa fa-file-image" aria-hidden="true"></i> File Manager</a>
    <div class="dropdown-menu">
      <a class="dropdown-item" href="#">All Files</a>
      <a class="dropdown-item" href="#">Add New File</a>
      <a class="dropdown-item" href="#">Edit File</a>
    </div>
  </li>
  <li class="nav-item dropdown dropdown-tree btn-group">
    <a class="nav-link dropdown-toggle" data-toggle="dropdown" href="#" role="button" aria-haspopup="true" aria-expanded="false"><i class="fa fa-file" aria-hidden="true"></i> Pages</a>
    <div class="dropdown-menu">
      <a class="dropdown-item" href="#">All Files</a>
      <a class="dropdown-item" href="#">Add New File</a>
      <a class="dropdown-item" href="#">Edit File</a>
    </div>
  </li>
```

```
<li class="nav-item dropdown dropdown-tree btn-group">
    <a class="nav-link dropdown-toggle" data-toggle="dropdown" href="#"
role="button" aria-haspopup="true" aria-expanded="false"><i class="fa fa-
thumbtack" aria-hidden="true"></i> Posts</a>
    <div class="dropdown-menu">
      <a class="dropdown-item" href="#">All Posts</a>
      <a class="dropdown-item" href="#">Add New Post</a>
      <a class="dropdown-item" href="#">Edit Post</a>
    </div>
  </li>
  <li class="nav-item">
    <a class="nav-link" href="#"><i class="fa fa-calendar" aria-
hidden="true"></i> Events</a>
  </li>
</ul>
<!-- /.nav -->
```

Step 9

Next, copy the page title and alert content and paste it inside the `.col .main`
content div.

Copy this code
https://bootstrapcreative.com/b4ap09

```
<h2>Dashboard<small> - Good morning Jacob.</small></h2>
<div class="alert alert-warning" role="alert">
  <button type="button" class="close" data-dismiss="alert" aria-label="Close">
    <span aria-hidden="true">&times;</span>
  </button>
  <strong>Update</strong> You have three unpublished drafts. <a href="">Edit</
a>
</div>
<!-- /.alert -->
```

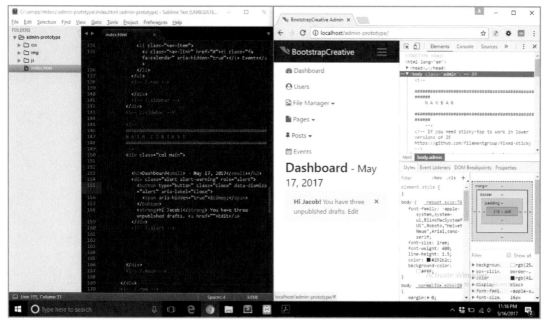

Your screen should now look like this.

Step 10

Next, copy the card deck content and paste it below the alert code you just added inside the `.col` `.main` content div.

Copy this code
https://bootstrapcreative.com/b4ap10

```
<!-- Card Deck Charts -->
<div class="card-deck">
  <div class="card">
    <div class="card-body">
      <h4 class="card-title">Traffic</h4>
      <canvas id="chartLine"></canvas>
    </div>
  </div>
```

```
<div class="card">
  <div class="card-body">
    <h4 class="card-title">Leads</h4>
      <canvas id="chartBar" ></canvas>
  </div>
</div>
<div class="card">
  <div class="card-body">
    <h4 class="card-title">Content</h4>
    <canvas id="chartPie"></canvas>
  </div>
</div>
</div>
<!-- /.card-deck -->
```

Step 11

Next, copy the card with a table inside it and paste it below the card deck you just added inside the `.col .main` content div.

Copy this code
https://bootstrapcreative.com/b4ap11

```
<!-- Content Edit Table -->
<div class="card mt-3">
  <div class="card-body">
    <h4>Recent Activity</h4>
    <table class="table table-responsive d-md-table">
      <thead>
        <tr>
          <th colspan="2">Title</th>
          <th>Author</th>
          <th>Date</th>
          <th>Type</th>
          <th>Action</th>
        </tr>
```

```
    </thead>
    <tbody>
      <tr class="bg-faded">
        <td scope="row">1</td>
        <td>Is Your Responsive Site Painfully Slow on Mobile? <small>Draft</
small></td>
        <td>Jacob Lett</td>
        <td>2/4/19</td>
        <td>Post</td>
        <td class="no-wrap"><a href=""><i class="fa fa-pencil pr-1"></
i>Edit</a> | <a href=""><i class="fa fa-trash pr-1"></i>Delete</a></td>
      </tr>
      <tr>
        <td scope="row">2</td>
        <td>How to Use Google Analytics Event Goals as AdWords Conversions</
td>
        <td>Sam Tryherhee</td>
        <td>2/12/19</td>
        <td>Post</td>
        <td><a href=""><i class="fa fa-pencil pr-1"></i>Edit</a> | <a
href=""><i class="fa fa-trash pr-1"></i>Delete</a></td>
      </tr>
      <tr>
        <td scope="row">3</td>
        <td>How we increased our blog's readership by 45% in three months</
td>
        <td>Jacob Lett</td>
        <td>2/22/19</td>
        <td>Post</td>
        <td><a href=""><i class="fa fa-pencil pr-1"></i>Edit</a> | <a
href=""><i class="fa fa-trash pr-1"></i>Delete</a></td>
      </tr>
      <tr>
        <td scope="row">4</td>
        <td>Going responsive helped CompanyX grow their organic search
traffic by 45%</td>
        <td>Zig Ziglar</td>
        <td>3/2/19</td>
        <td>Post</td>
        <td><a href=""><i class="fa fa-pencil pr-1"></i>Edit</a> | <a
href=""><i class="fa fa-trash pr-1"></i>Delete</a></td>
      </tr>
```

```
      <tr>
        <td scope="row">5</td>
        <td>About Us</td>
        <td>Sam Tryherhee</td>
        <td>3/2/19</td>
        <td>Page</td>
        <td><a href=""><i class="fa fa-pencil pr-1"></i>Edit</a> | <a
href=""><i class="fa fa-trash pr-1"></i>Delete</a></td>
      </tr>
      <tr>
        <td scope="row">6</td>
        <td>Services</td>
        <td>Jacob Lett</td>
        <td>4/12/19</td>
        <td>Page</td>
        <td><a href=""><i class="fa fa-pencil pr-1"></i>Edit</a> | <a
href=""><i class="fa fa-trash pr-1"></i>Delete</a></td>
      </tr>
    </tbody>
  </table>
 </div>
</div>
<!-- /.card -->
```

Step 12

Next, copy the footer content and paste it below the cards you just added inside the `.col .main` content div.

> **Copy this code**
> https://bootstrapcreative.com/b4ap12

```
<!--
##################################################
F O O T E R
##################################################
-->
<footer class="footer py-3">
  <div class="container-fluid">
    <a href="//BootstrapCreative.com">© BootstrapCreative</a>
  </div>
</footer>
```

Summary

Great job. You now have a working dashboard using Bootstrap 4. We used Bootstrap's default styles to get a working prototype to quickly demonstrate functionality.
The prototype gets the basic idea down but it doesn't look very good.

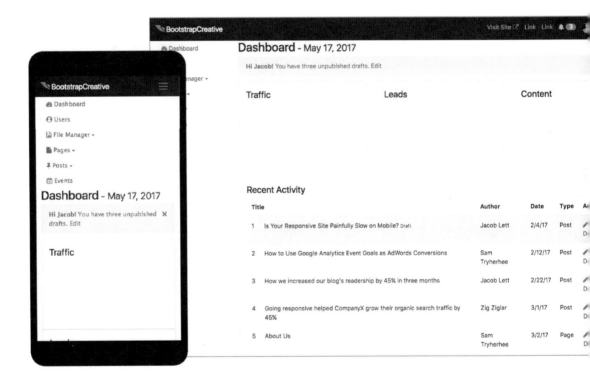

Customize the Design
Where to Start

If we refer back to the design process we are now in the design phase. In this phase, we will explore design options and then begin to build a clickable design that we can use for testing and approval.

Design Exploration

Now that you have an approved wireframe, architecture, and page content you can begin exploring different visual solutions. Every designer has their own method but I recommend sketching with paper and pencil first.

It is easier to flush out multiple ideas on paper than it is to draw shapes in a design program. Also, if it doesn't work as a sketch it will never work as a final design.

Once you have a sketch you like you can then move to a design program like Photoshop, Adobe XD, or Sketch. These apps will help you work out aesthetics, colors, typography, spacing, and graphics before writing any code. Some designers skip this step and go right to code and design in the browser. I personally think this limits your creativity especially if you use Bootstrap. **The UI of Bootstrap should not influence your design**. Following this progression will greatly reduce the chances of your site looking too much like a Bootstrap site.

Since design is such a broad topic and would require a lot of explanation I am going to skip past this process and move right to development.

Clickable Design

Before responsive design, it was much easier to convert a desktop design and convert it to code because everything was fixed width and not much would change.

Today we have to design for different breakpoints, devices, and bandwidths. All with their own set of nuances and challenges. Because of this, I recommend never showing a client a flat design. You want to make sure they see the site on different devices as well.

Ok, let's look at how we are going to change the design.

The time it takes to make a decision increases as the number of alternatives increases.
— *William Edmund Hick*

Add a
dismissable alert

Convert the default
dropdown items to be
a navigation tree that
toggles sub items
when clicked

Sidebar to always be
100% height

Add responsive
data charts

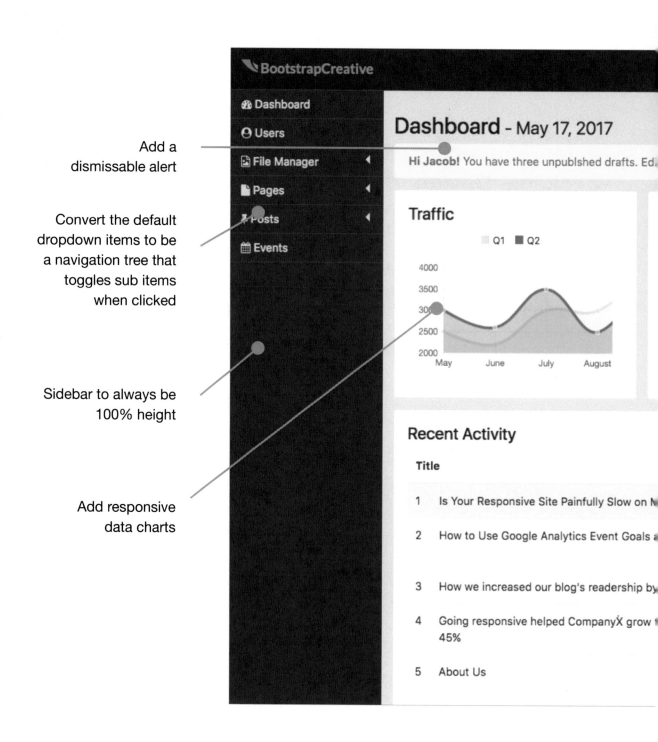

BootstrapCreative

Dashboard
Users
File Manager
Pages
Posts
Events

Dashboard - May 17, 2017

Hi Jacob! You have three unpublshed drafts. Ed

Traffic

Q1 Q2

4000
3500
300
2500
2000
May   June   July   August

Recent Activity

Title

1   Is Your Responsive Site Painfully Slow on N

2   How to Use Google Analytics Event Goals

3   How we increased our blog's readership by

4   Going responsive helped CompanyX grow
     45%

5   About Us

Step 1

In order to override the default Bootstrap styles, we have to reference our own CSS and JS files placed **after the Bootstrap files**. The browser loads the page from the top down, so our styles will change what the browser was told to do by Bootstrap because they are listed after it.

First, copy some branding stylesheets and paste them in the CSS comment section right before the closing </head> tag. We are adding the Lato Google Font and admin.css custom stylesheet.

Copy this code
https://bootstrapcreative.com/b4ad01

```
<!-- Lato Display Font from Google Fonts -->
<link href="https://fonts.googleapis.com/css?family=Lato:400,400i,700,700i"
rel="stylesheet">
<!-- Custom styles for this template -->
<link href="css/admin.css" rel="stylesheet">
```

Step 2

Now, copy some branding scripts and paste them in the JS comment section right before the closing </body> tag.

We are adding the Chart.js plugin for the graphs and admin.js for any custom scripts.

Copy this code
https://bootstrapcreative.com/b4ad02

```
<!-- Custom Javascript -->
<script src="https://cdnjs.cloudflare.com/ajax/libs/Chart.js/2.7.3/Chart.min.
js" crossorigin="anonymous"></script>
<script src="js/admin.js"></script>
```

Step 3

Open `admin.css` and copy and paste the placeholder comment sections.

Copy this code
https://bootstrapcreative.com/b4ad03

```
/*
BootstrapCreative
Created by: Jacob Lett
Licensed MIT
2019

1 rem    = 16px
.75 rem  = 12px
.5 rem   = 8px
.25 rem  = 4px

Bootstrap 4 breakpoints
@media (min-width: 576px) { }
@media (min-width: 768px) { }
@media (min-width: 992px) { }
@media (min-width: 1200px) { }

Colors
#0275d8 - primary blue
#636c72 - light gray
#292b2c - black
*/


/*
```

```
####################################################
G R I D  &  T Y P E
####################################################
*/

/*
####################################################
C O M P O N E N T S
####################################################
*/
/*
::::::::::::::::::::::::::::::::::::::::::::::::::::::
Navbar
*/

/*
::::::::::::::::::::::::::::::::::::::::::::::::::::::
Sidebar Dropdown
*/

/*
::::::::::::::::::::::::::::::::::::::::::::::::::::::
Card deck
*/

/*
::::::::::::::::::::::::::::::::::::::::::::::::::::::
Table
*/

/*
::::::::::::::::::::::::::::::::::::::::::::::::::::::
Charts
*/
```

I added some common reference there like rem to pixels, breakpoints, and brand colors. I also have two main sections: Grid & Type, and Components. If you purchased the Pro package, the *Web Design Primer* mentions organizing your CSS styles by component instead of by page. So we will be following this format.

Step 4

Next, copy some global styles to change the body background color and make the main container 100% height. This prevents the sidebar from looking too short.

Copy this code
https://bootstrapcreative.com/b4ad04

```
/*
####################################################
G R I D  &  T Y P E
####################################################
*/

body {
    background: #e2e2e2;
}

/* makes the sidebar 100% height */
html,
body,
.container-fluid {height: 100%;}
.main {min-height: 100vh;}
```

Step 5

Next, copy the navbar component styles and paste it below the navbar comment section. This will change the link color and add a blue bottom border to the navbar.

Copy this code
https://bootstrapcreative.com/b4ad05

```
/*
::::::::::::::::::::::::::::::::::::::::::::::::::::::
navbar
*/
.navbar-brand {
  font-family: 'Lato', sans-serif;
  font-weight: 700;
}
.navbar-brand span {
  color: #89969e;
}
.navbar {
  border-bottom:2px solid #0275d8;
}
```

Step 6

Next, copy the sidebar navigation styles and paste it below the Sidebar Dropdown comment section. These styles will convert the dropdowns into a tree menu.

Copy this code
https://bootstrapcreative.com/b4ad06

```
/*
::::::::::::::::::::::::::::::::::::::::::::::::::::::
Sidebar Dropdown
*/

/* add some space so it does not touch the navbar */
.sidebar, .main {padding-top:2em;}

.sidebar {
  background-color: #373a3c;
  border-right: 1px solid #eee;
  padding:0;
}
```

```css
.sidebar .nav a {
  padding:.5rem 1rem;
  color:#e2e2e2;
}

.dropdown-tree .dropdown-toggle::after {
  position: absolute;
  right:20px;
  top:10px;
}

.sidebar .nav-item, .navbar {
  border-bottom:1px solid #555;
}

.sidebar .dropdown-menu a:hover {
  color: #373a3c;
}

/* Customize the sidebar dropdown to be a navigation tree */
.dropdown-tree {flex-direction:column;}
.dropdown-tree .dropdown-item {
  white-space: normal;
  padding:3px 0;
}

.dropdown-tree .dropdown-menu {
  /* important is needed to override inline styles applied by Bootstrap JS */
  position: relative!important;
  transform:none!important;
  top: 100%;
  left: 0;
  float: none;
  min-width: 0;
  padding: 0px;
  margin: 0px;
  font-size: 1rem;
  color: #373a3c;
  text-align: left;
  list-style: none;
  background-color: #555;
```

```
    border: none;
  }

  .dropdown-tree .dropdown-toggle::after {
    display: inline-block;
    width: 0;
    height: 0;
    margin-left: .3em;
    vertical-align: middle;
    content: "";
    border:none;
    border-top: .4em solid transparent;
    border-right: .4em solid;
    border-bottom: .4em solid  transparent;
    border-left: .4em solid  transparent;
  }

  .dropdown-tree.show .dropdown-toggle::after {
    margin-top:3px;
    display: inline-block;
    margin-left: 10px;
    border-top: .4em solid ;
    border-right: .4em solid transparent;
  }
```

Step 7

The default styles for the Card Deck have a wide margin and I would like it to be narrower. Also, I am going to add a media query so I can control how the columns break on mobile breakpoints. Currently, the last column goes 100% width.

Next, copy the card deck styles and paste them below the Card Deck comment section.

Copy this code
https://bootstrapcreative.com/b4ad07

```css
/*
:::::::::::::::::::::::::::::::::::::::::::::::::::::::
Card deck
*/
.card-deck .card {
  margin-bottom: 1rem;
}

/* Set width to make card deck cards 100% width */
@media (max-width: 768px) {

  .card-deck .card {
    flex-direction: column;
    -webkit-box-flex: 1 1 auto;
    -webkit-flex: 1 1 auto;
    -ms-flex: 1 1 auto;
    flex: 1 1 auto;
    margin-bottom: 1rem;
  }

}
.admin .card-deck .card:last-child {
  margin-bottom: 0rem;
}
```

```
@media (min-width: 769px) {

  .card-deck .card {
  margin-bottom: 0rem;
  }

  /* Make the space between cards less wide */
  .admin .card-deck .card {
  margin-left:15px;
  margin-right:0px;
  }
  .admin .card-deck .card:last-child {
  margin-right:15px;
  }

}
```

Step 8

See how the Delete link under the Action heading wraps leaving the icon on the line above? Let's prevent wrapping on the last table cell.

Copy the table styles and paste them below the table comment section.

Copy this code
https://bootstrapcreative.com/b4ad08

```
/*
::::::::::::::::::::::::::::::::::::::::::::::::::::::
Card deck
*/

.card-deck .card {
  margin-bottom: 1rem;
}
```

```
/* Set width to make card deck cards 100% width */
@media (max-width: 768px) {

  .card-deck .card {
    flex-direction: column;
    -webkit-box-flex: 1 1 auto;
    -webkit-flex: 1 1 auto;
    -ms-flex: 1 1 auto;
    flex: 1 1 auto;
    margin-bottom: 1rem;
  }

}

.admin .card-deck .card:last-child {
  margin-bottom: 0rem;
}

@media (min-width: 769px) {

  .card-deck .card {
  margin-bottom: 0rem;
  }

  /* Make the space between cards less wide */
  .admin .card-deck .card {
  margin-left:15px;
  margin-right:0px;
  }
  .admin .card-deck .card:last-child {
  margin-right:15px;
  }

}
```

Step 9

Open up `index.html` and look in the card deck code section and look at the HTML of one of the cards. You should see the code below.

```
<div id="line-legend" class="chart-legend"></div>
<canvas id="myGraph"></canvas>
```

The Chart.js will replace these elements with the graphs. We first need to initiate the plugin and give it some data to work with.

Next, copy the javascript code and paste it inside the `admin.js` file.

Copy this code
https://bootstrapcreative.com/b4ad09

```
console.log('admin.js loaded');

// BEGIN Line Graph ==========================================
var chartLine = {
  type: 'line',
  data: {
    labels: ['May', 'June', 'July', 'August'],
    datasets: [{
      label: 'Q1',
      backgroundColor: 'rgba(0, 0, 0, 0.1)',
      borderColor: 'rgba(0, 0, 0, 0.2)',
      data: [1900, 1800, 1900, 1800],
      fill: true,
    }, {
      label: 'Q2',
      fill: true,
      backgroundColor: 'rgba(0, 123, 255, 0.7)',
      borderColor: 'rgba(0, 123, 255, 1)',
      data: [2000, 1700, 2000, 1500],
    }]
  },
```

```
  options: {
    responsive: true,
    title: {
      display: false,
      text: 'Line Chart'
    },
    tooltips: {
      mode: 'index',
      intersect: false,
    },
    hover: {
      mode: 'nearest',
      intersect: true
    },
    scales: {
      xAxes: [{
        display: true,
        scaleLabel: {
          display: true,
          labelString: 'Month'
        }
      }],
      yAxes: [{
        display: true,

        scaleLabel: {
          display: true,
          labelString: 'Views'
        }
      }]
    }
  }
};

// BEGIN Bar Graph ========================================
var chartBar = {
  type: 'bar',
  data: {
    labels: ["Sun", "Mon", "Tue", "Wed", "Thu", "Fri", "Sat"],
    datasets: [{
        label: 'Last Week',
```

```
            data: [1, 2, 3, 4, 5, 6, 7],
            backgroundColor: [
              'rgba(0, 0, 0, .2)',
              'rgba(0, 0, 0, .2)',
              'rgba(0, 0, 0, .2)',
              'rgba(0, 0, 0, .2)',
              'rgba(0, 0, 0, .2)',
              'rgba(0, 0, 0, .2)',
              'rgba(0, 0, 0, .2)',
            ]
          },
          {
            label: 'This Week',
            data: [2, 4, 6, 8, 10, 12, 14],
            backgroundColor: [
              'rgba(0, 123, 255, 1)',
              'rgba(0, 123, 255, 1)',
              'rgba(0, 123, 255, 1)',
              'rgba(0, 123, 255, 1)',
              'rgba(0, 123, 255, 1)',
              'rgba(0, 123, 255, 1)',
              'rgba(0, 123, 255, 1)'
            ]
          }
        ]
      },
      options: {
        scales: {
          yAxes: [{
            ticks: {
              beginAtZero: true
            }
          }]
        }
      }
    }
};

// BEGIN Pie Graph ==============================================
var chartPie = {
  type: 'pie',
  data: {
```

```
      labels: ['Drafts', 'Pages', 'Posts'],
      datasets: [{
        label: 'Q1',
        backgroundColor: [
          'rgba(0, 0, 0, 0.2)',
          'rgba(0, 123, 255, 0.7)',
          'rgba(0, 123, 255, 1)'
        ],
        data: [5, 15, 25],
        fill: true,
        borderWidth: 0
      }]
    },
    options: {
      responsive: true,
      title: {
        display: false,
        text: 'Pie Chart'
      },
      tooltips: {
        mode: 'index',
        intersect: false,
      },
      hover: {
        mode: 'nearest',
        intersect: true
      },
      scales: {
        xAxes: [{
          display: false
        }],
        yAxes: [{
          display: false
        }]
      }
    }
};
// Load Chart.js Graphs after the window is fully loaded
window.onload = function () {
  var ctxLine = document.getElementById('chartLine').getContext('2d');
  window.chartLine = new Chart(ctxLine, chartLine);
```

```
var ctxBar = document.getElementById('chartBar').getContext('2d');
window.chartBar = new Chart(ctxBar, chartBar);

var ctxPie = document.getElementById('chartPie').getContext('2d');
window.chartPie = new Chart(ctxPie, chartPie);
};
```

Step 10 *Final Step*

Awesome! The charts are loading in now... but it doesn't look very good. They are way too wide. We need to add some styles to control their sizing.

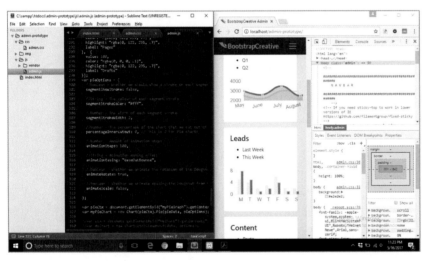

Charts break the layout so some custom styles are needed.

Next, copy the charts styles and paste them below the Charts comment section.

```
/*
::::::::::::::::::::::::::::::::::::::::::::::::::::::
Charts
*/

/* makes chart responsive */
canvas {
  padding: 15px;
  width: 100%!important;
  height: auto!important;
}

/* legend styles */
.chart-legend {
  margin:0;
  width:100%;
  text-align: center;
}
.chart-legend ul {width:100%;margin:0;padding:0;}
.chart-legend li {
  list-style-type: none;
  padding:0;
  font-size:14px;
  display: inline-block;
  margin:0 1rem 0 0;
}
.chart-legend li span{
  display: inline-block;
  width: 12px;
  height: 12px;
  margin-right: 5px;
}
```

The completed design

Summary

Great job. The customization of the dashboard demonstrates how you can leverage existing component library and push their customization to reach your intended design. If the components are not working, you may have to build a new one from scratch.

The important thing to remember, if you want your design to influence the default Bootstrap styles and not have Bootstrap styles influence your design. This will help you use it as a starting point that you build upon and not as your designer.

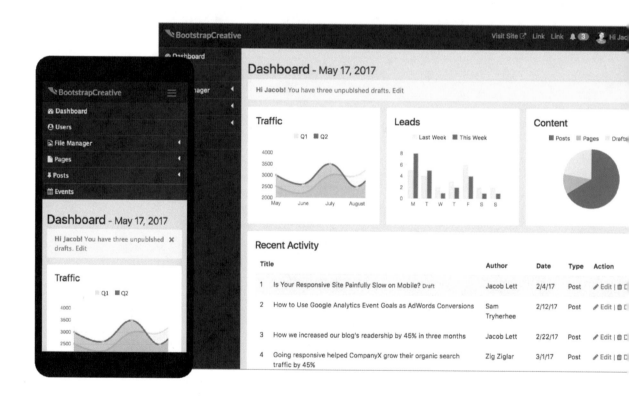

Responsive Layout Tips

Introduction

This chapter is a collection of common questions and tips to help you address common responsive layout challenges

Content precedes design. Design in the absence of content is not design, it's decoration.

—— Jeffrey Zeldman

How does CSS flexbox work?

How to Take Command of CSS Flexbox

As a kid I loved playing with toy plastic army men. I would line them up and pretend to be in command giving orders to my soldiers in order to defeat the enemy. Since I was in full command, the soldiers would look to me for their orders.

Sometimes a hot shot recruit would overstep my orders and go rogue, He would ignore and override my orders and just do what he wanted.

My example demonstrates the basic principle of the CSS display property flexbox which is…

Flex items (soldiers) follow the orders given by their flex container (commander).

In addition, an individual flex item has the ability to override the orders given out by the flex container if required. All it needs is a unique class name or ID with a unique set of properties.

In this flexbox tutorial, I will be answering some of the most common questions and show you how to start using flexbox in your projects.

What is flexbox?

Flexbox is a CSS display property that was introduced in CSS3. If you are familiar with an UL and LI relationship in HTML unordered lists, flexbox is very similar to how it has sub-items or children inside a parent wrapping container. With flexbox they are called flex items.

The parent-child relationship of an unordered list

```
<ul>
  <li>list item</li>
  <li>list item</li>
</ul>
```

Is like the parent-child relationship of a flexbox container and it's flexbox items

```
<div class="your-class">
  <div>flex item</div>
  <div>flex item</div>
</div>
```

But you're flex items do not have to be the same type of HTML element. In this example, I use different HTML elements but the first children still act as flex items.

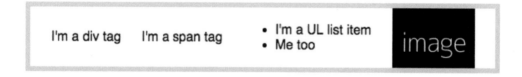

Since flexbox is a display property, it can be applied to any parent and child HTML elements and does not need to have its own HTML element like `<flexbox>`.

When and why would you use flexbox instead of floats?

The demands of web page layout have often exceeded what was currently available. Early websites used HTML tables for page layout and were then replaced by floats. But even floats were not intended for complex page layout. Their purpose is to keep an image in the text flow but allow you to float it to the right or the left and have text flow around it. Very similar to what you would see in a book or magazine.

Floats were intended to keep images inline with the copy but have text flow around them. Similar to what you would find in traditional print layouts.

The main reason why you would use flexbox today instead of floats is to satisfy the demands of responsive design.

Flexbox gives you the ability to change the order and alignment of elements with media queries. So you could have your last column listed first on mobile.

You would need to use javascript to achieve this same level of control in a float based layout.

How does flexbox work?

Flex Container (commanding officer)

Flex layout gives the container the ability to alter its items' width/height (and order) to best fill the available space of the container.

The container has a main axis and cross axis which depends on the flex direction. Each axis has a start and end.

For example, if you set the flex direction to the column. The main axis is vertical and the cross axis is horizontal. If you set the flex direction to row, the main axis is horizontal and the cross axis is vertical.

Default order of items

flex-direction: row

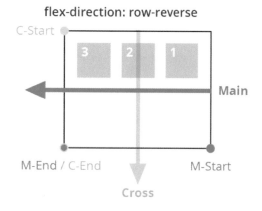

flex-direction: column

flex-direction: column (diagram)

Reverse the order of items

flex-direction: row-reverse

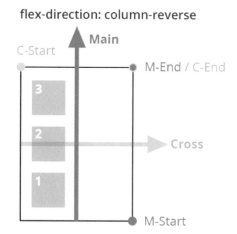

flex-direction: column-reverse

Ok now to discuss the flex items inside the container.

Flex Item (individual soldier)

Flexbox items are like soldiers because they follow the orders given by their container. Just like soldiers listen to their commanding officer in battle.

By default, flex items all want to appear on the same line.

Individual flexbox items (soldiers) can be targeted with a unique class and property to override the orders given by their container.

The example below uses the class `.rogue-flex-item` to make adjustments to only Soldier J in red.

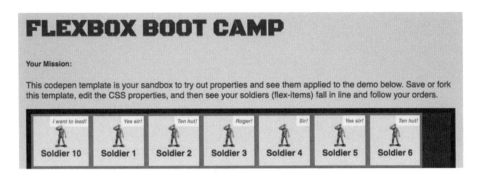

Your turn! You can fork this example on codepen[1] and use as a template for trying out flexbox on your own.

How do you enable and use flexbox?

Enabling flexbox is just like declaring an image to be block or inline-block. You just need to have some HTML markup with some child elements and a class name.

```
<div class="your-class">
  <div>flex item</div>
  <div>flex item</div>
</div>
```

---

1   https://codepen.io/JacobLett/pen/xXQVPV/

Then in your CSS file, target your class and write `display:flex`

```
.your-class {
  /* If you just have display:flex the flex items will act like inline items */
  display:flex;
  /* determines the main and cross axis */
  flex-direction:column;
}
```

Now that you have flexbox enabled and set the main and cross axis, you can now give more detailed commands on how you want your items to behave. You can view the full list of flexbox properties available on my **flexbox cheat sheet reference page**[2].

How do you make flexbox responsive with Bootstrap 4?

In my example I have three flex items and I would like to have the last item to appear first only on mobile vertical orientation. Since I am working mobile first, I would need to list my flex items in the source order I want them to appear in mobile. So 3, 1, 2.

I will then use CSS to change the order at the breakpoint above what I am targeting. So my media query below is saying, "don't apply this until the window is at least 575px wide".

---

2   https://bootstrapcreative.com/resources/flexbox-cheat-sheet/

```
@media (min-width: 575px) {
  .rogue-flex-item  {
    order:3;
  }
}
```

Since Bootstrap has a set of pre-defined CSS styles we will do most of our work in the HTML document adding the necessary classes.

```
<h2>Bootstrap 4 Flexbox Classes</h2>
<div class="d-flex flex-row justify-content-start flex-wrap">
  <div class="order-sm-3">Soldier 3 <small>I want to lead!</small></div>
  <div class="order-sm-1">Soldier 1 <small>Yes sir!</small></div>
  <div class="order-sm-2">Soldier 2 <small>Ten hut!</small></div>
</div>
<!-- /.flex-container -->
```

Conclusion

Flexbox is powerful and it's fundamental to understanding how the Bootstrap 4 grid works. The main advantage flexbox has over float based layouts is re-ordering items. The three main components of flexbox are the flex container, flex items, and main/cross axis. The remaining properties build on that foundation. Get a free flexbox cheat sheet pdf[3] to help you reference all of the properties.

---

3   https://bootstrapcreative.com/resources/flexbox-cheat-sheet/

How do I prevent a full-width carousel from being so tall on desktop?

Do you want your Bootstrap carousel to extend the full width of the browser window? Do your images look cut off or have unwanted padding on the left and right? In this tutorial, we will take a closer look at the Bootstrap 4 carousel and determine the best approach to making it full width and responsive.

The Problem

If you use the carousel code snippet from the Bootstrap 4 documentation you will notice the carousel anchor links do not wrap the entire image. In most cases, you will probably want the opposite. So for this example, I am going to make this adjustment to the code.

Each image has the `.img-fluid` class which tells the browser to only scale the image down if it does not fit in the smaller width. But for wide windows, it doesn't scale up. But since you want to go full width, your images will appear cut off on really large screens.

```
.img-fluid {
    max-width: 100%;
    height: auto;
}
```

In order to fix this, you will need to add the CSS rule below to your stylesheet to force your carousel image to always be full width. I first tried `height:auto;` so the image height would stay in the right proportion. But that did not work because the parent element `.carousel-item` is set to `display:flex`. Changing the height to 100% fixed this.

```
/*
Forces carousel image to be 100% width and not max width of 100%
*/
.carousel-item .img-fluid {
  width:100%;
  height:100%;
}
```

This approach forces you to choose the widest image size and then load it on mobile. This is not mobile friendly because it dramatically decreases page load speed because the images have a large file size (more pixels = more load time). One of the most common causes of slow websites is large images, so we will want to correct this in our final solution.

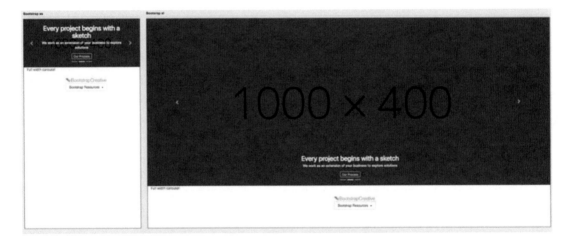

Above, notice how the carousel looks super small on mobile and HUGE on wide desktops? This doesn't look right.

In the next section we will improve the following:

- Improve the load speed by serving the right sized image at the right breakpoint
- Fix the layout aesthetics of the image sizes being too small or too large

View demo of the problem example: https://codepen.io/JacobLett/full/PjKLgK/

The Solution

HTML5 has introduced two different ways to handle responsive images: the `picture` element and `srcset` img attribute. Img srcset lets you specify different image resolutions based on window size and pixel density of the screen. This solves the page load problem but would not be able to make the xs and xl image proportions look better. We want the mobile image to be square and the desktop image to be a rectangle so we need more "art direction" control on what image is used and when.

The picture tag is designed for this scenario, so we will use this instead.

Keep in mind, you will need to use a picturefill script[4] to support IE11 and below because these versions do not support the picture tag.

Below is an example of the picture tag with different images specified. See how each image source has a media query similar to CSS media queries? Following mobile first, the image tag loads the smallest image first and then swaps it out on larger sizes (smallest to biggest from the bottom up). This will improve page load significantly on mobile because it loads an image at a pixel resolution suitable for its screen size. Plus it gives you way more control of how things look at different breakpoints.

```
<picture>
  <source srcset="https://dummyimage.com/2000x400/007aeb/4196e5" media="(min-width: 1400px)">
  <source srcset="https://dummyimage.com/1400x400/007aeb/4196e5" media="(min-width: 768px)">
  <source srcset="https://dummyimage.com/800x400/007aeb/4196e5" media="(min-width: 576px)">
  <img srcset="https://dummyimage.com/600x400/007aeb/4196e5" alt="responsive image" class="d-block img-fluid">
</picture>
```

---

4   https://scottjehl.github.io/picturefill/

When setting up the image sizes and media size breakpoints, I referenced this list of most common screen resolutions[5]. The second highest desktop screen size is 1920 x 1080 so I wanted to make sure i could cover that width without making the image blurry. So we are only going to load this if the image is greater than 1400px. Make the necessary adjustments based on your site analytics to target the most common screen resolutions.

Looking good. The xs breakpoint is square and the xl is a wide rectangle. Maximizing the space and making the carousel more mobile friendly.

View the final solution: https://codepen.io/JacobLett/full/weqOjq

Things to watch out for

- Since you want your carousel to extend to the edges, keep your carousel outside of a `.container` or `.container-fluid` class because this applies left and right padding.

- Using the picture element for your images requires a lot more image editing in Adobe Photoshop or similar software. If a creative change is made it will have to be applied to multiple image versions. So this will take more time.

- Using placeholder images first can help figure out image sizes and breakpoints before you do any final image cropping.

---

5   http://gs.statcounter.com/screen-resolution-stats/desktop/worldwide

Summary

In this tutorial, you learned how to customize the carousel code snippet to use responsive images and go full width. This optimization achieves better load times on mobile and gives the designer control on how the images look at the various breakpoints.

The only downsides are that it requires more image editing time and needs a polyfill to support IE11 and below. But in my opinion, the pros greatly outweigh the cons. The breakpoint preview screenshots used in this tutorial were created using Robin available in the Bootstrap 4 Toolkit[6].

srcset if you're lazy, picture if you're crazy
—— Mat Marquis

6   https://bootstrapcreative.com/b4toolkit

How do I change the order of columns on mobile?

With Bootstrap 4 column ordering[7] it is best to start out understanding how the natural or default column ordering works. When your browser reads your HTML code it reads from the top and works its way down reading left to right. So in a two column grid, the first column will be the first one it finds under the .row class.

```
<h2>Without column ordering</h2>
<div class="row">
  <div class="col-sm-6">
    <img src="https://dummyimage.com/400x400/000/fff&text=A" alt="" class="w-100" />
  </div>                              Column A
  <div class="col-sm-6">
    <img src="https://dummyimage.com/400x400/000/fff&text=B" alt="" class="w-100" />
  </div>                              Column B
</div>
```

Remember to Write Your Code "Mobile First"

What is mobile first? It basically means the HTML and CSS you first send to the browser are for mobile devices. So you should write your HTML markup in the order you want it to appear on mobile. Then use the order classes to rearrange things on larger devices like a forklift moves boxes around.

The result

A two column grid with the images 100% width of the column. Since each column has a class `.col-sm-6`, each column will be 100% width on mobile.

---

7   https://getbootstrap.com/docs/4.0/layout/grid/#reordering

Now, how would you make the B column swap positions with A column on mobile?

So on mobile, it will be BA and on everything else, it will be AB.

To do this, you would need to set the source code to be in the order you want it to be on mobile. Then add the order classes to the columns specifying the order at the breakpoint you choose. In our case, we want SM and up. Using Bootstrap's order classes you can essentially move columns around like a forklift.

```
<h2>With column ordering</h2>
  <div class="row">
    <div class="col-sm-6 order-sm-12">
      <img src="https://dummyimage.com/400x400/000/fff&text=B" alt=""
class="w-100" />
    </div>
    <div class="col-sm-6 order-sm-1">
      <img src="https://dummyimage.com/400x400/000/fff&text=A" alt=""
class="w-100" />
    </div>
  </div>
```

.order-sm-12

Add this class to the first column to push it to the last position to the right. Remember Bootstrap is based on a 12 point grid system.

.order-sm-1

Now add this class to the second column to move the column to the left starting position.

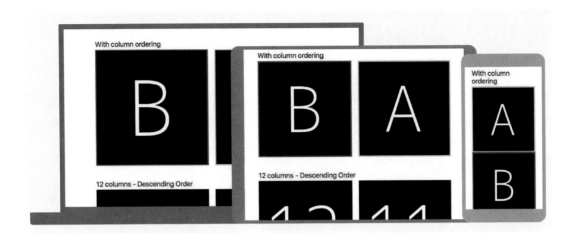

How does this work?

Bootstrap 4 uses CSS flexbox for the grid system. So the column ordering essentially applies an order property to the flex item you are moving.

Conclusion

The most important thing to remember is the Bootstrap CSS Framework is mobile first. Write your markup how you want it to be displayed on mobile devices then apply classes if you need to change things at higher breakpoints.

Then apply the `.order-*` classes to reorder things at different breakpoints. Always keeping in mind your classes need to add up to 12 columns. You can experiment with this code in the demo found here https://codepen.io/JacobLett/pen/xRadPZ

How do I change the default colors and fonts?

A common Bootstrap customization request is changing the default color scheme and fonts. You have a few options depending on how you are using Bootstrap in your project.

1. CSS Overrides

If you are linking to a pre-compiled version of Bootstrap I recommend looking at the raw source and using search and replace in your code text editor to replace all of the color values. Then save this new stylesheet in your project folder and link to your customized version instead of the CDN version.

If you are worried about missing future updates and having to repeat the process each time. You could follow the same steps as above but delete everything except your color changes. It will take some cleanup work but now you will have a new file you can call `bootstrap-color.css` that only contains your new color declarations. Then link to the new stylesheet after the CDN version to override the default colors.

Change the default font to a Google font

Add the Google font link to the <head> of your document

```
<link href='http://fonts.googleapis.com/css?family=Oswald:400,300,700'
rel='stylesheet' type='text/css'>
```

Add this to your `custom.css` file to override the base font family

```
body {
  font-family: 'Oswald', sans-serif !important;
}
```

2. Compiling Source – Update Sass variables

For more control, I recommend using the source files and updating the Bootstrap color variables. Then convert your SCSS to CSS using your build process. If you are new to SCSS and want to learn how to compile a custom version of Bootstrap check out my course[8] that covers this topic in more detail.

3. Hybrid – Use Whootstrap

Whootstrap[9] is an online tool that lets you modify the Bootstrap Sass variables and save out a compiled CSS theme file for your project. So instead of having to use the command line, you can do it all right in the browser. This tool is essentially a hybrid approach of the previous two options. The only thing I don't like is how you are dependent on a third-party to keep the code up to date. Compiling your own version like option 2 above ensures you are always referencing the latest code.

---

8   https://bootstrapcreative.com/learnsass
9   http://whootstrap.themes.guide/

Can I adjust text size with Bootstrap in a responsive design?

Since Bootstrap is a "Mobile First" CSS framework you need to write your styles mobile up. So, your smallest bold font size will be written outside of a media query and then you will make adjustments as the viewport gets larger. There isn't a class already set up in Bootstrap for this so you have to write custom CSS rules.

In the example code below, we are changing the h1 font size to 16px and enlarging it as the screen gets wider. You would follow this same pattern for other text you would like to make adjustments to.

Code demo: https://codepen.io/JacobLett/pen/VpvKWg

```
/*
Extra small devices (portrait phones, less than 544px)
No media query since this is the default in Bootstrap because it is "mobile
first"
*/
h1 {font-size:1rem;} /*1rem = 16px*/


/*
:::::::::::::::::::::::::::::::::::::::::::::::::::::
Bootstrap 4 breakpoints
*/
/* Extra large devices (large desktops, 1200px and up) */
@media (min-width: 1200px) {
  h1 {font-size:3rem;} /*1rem = 16px*/
}
/*
Custom media queries
*/
/* Set width to make card deck cards 100% width */
@media (min-width: 950px) and (max-width:1100px) {
  h1 {font-size:2.75rem;color:red;}
}
```

Conclusion

Congratulations!

You made it to the end of the *Bootstrap 4 Quick Start*.

In this book, we covered the history of responsive web design and how Bootstrap helps make building responsive websites easier.

We then learned about the design process and how it is important in achieving a design that is functional and aesthetically pleasing. Bootstrap should never influence the UI of your site so it is always best to design on paper then in a graphics program like Sketch or Adobe XD/Photoshop. Once the initial design is complete a design prototype is created to make sure the client signs-off on code and not a flat file. This will prevent surprises to the client as well eliminate comments like "Why does this not match the .psd?"

What are you going to build next?

To your success,

P.S. If you found my book helpful, I would really appreciate a review letting others know how it has helped you. Or you can email me directly at jacoblett@bootstrapcreative.com.

Bootstrap 4 Toolkit

Want to improve your workflow and save time using Bootstrap 4? The Bootstrap 4 Toolkit includes tutorial vidoes, project template code files, responsive development tools, Photoshop grid templates, and printable reference guides.

Learn More: https://bootstrapcreative.com/b4toolkit

Bootstrap 4 Sass Quick Start

Want to learn how to modify Bootstrap 4 variables using NPM scripts? This video course will walk you through the steps of making your own custom Bootstrap 4 theme.

Learn More: https://bootstrapcreative.com/learnsass

Web Design Quick Start

Learn how to design a website from the very beginning. Focusing on design principles, typography, layout, color, UX and UI basics, and creating a mockup in Adobe XD.
Learn More: https://bootstrapcreative.com/learndesign

HTML, CSS, & JS Quick Start

A quick overview of the three primary languages of the web.
Learn More: https://bootstrapcreative.com/learnhtmlcss

You'll never know everything about anything, especially something you love.
— *Julia Child*

Anyone who stops learning is old, whether at twenty or eighty. Anyone who keeps learning stays young.
— *Henry Ford*

Appendix

Join the Community

Facebook Group - Web Design with Bootstrap CSS

When I started learning web design I had a lot of questions but I did not know anyone I could ask. **So I would go to forums like Stack Overflow and post my question but then get it gets blocked or deleted.** I hate to say it, but StackOverflow isn't very welcoming to beginners. So I created a friendly group for beginners and experienced designers and developers to connect and help each other learn.

Join the Group: https://www.facebook.com/groups/wdwbootstrap/

Online Chat Room - Spectrum

Join the chat room: https://spectrum.chat/bootstrapcreative

Other Places to Get Help

- **Bootstrap Slack:** https://getbootstrap.slack.com/
- **StackOverflow:** http://stackoverflow.com/questions/tagged/twitter-bootstrap
- **Quora:** https://www.quora.com/pinned/Bootstrap-CSS-Framework
- **CSS-Tricks Forum:** https://css-tricks.com/forums/

Web Hosting Recommendations

It can be hard finding a good web hosting company. I have had some good experiences and some really bad ones. You can see what I recommend at the page below.

https://bootstrapcreative.com/web-hosting/

Web Development Term Glossary

Adaptive Web Design

Another approach is to build multiple versions of a website and use server side detection to then present custom code for that device or viewport size.

You could decide to have your mobile site on a separate domain for example m.domain.com. The server will then automatically serve all mobile traffic to that domain. The server could also perform dynamic serving of page content so that you have just one domain name.

The downsides to this approach is it requires complex server side detection code and is harder to maintain multiple site versions.

Compile

In web development you often see the term compile which means to convert a higher level code (source code) to a lower level (distribution code). Often its LESS or Sass into CSS using a tool like Grunt, Gulp, or desktop application like codekit.

In node.js based projects you will often find a source folder containing all of the pre-compiled files like Sass. Then a distribution folder that contains all of the converted CSS code.

Component

The keyword in that phrase is **isolation**.

Since CSS cascades down to child elements how do you isolate things and write styles to target specific components and leave everything as is? The solution Bootstrap presented is the use of CSS classes with prefixes and distinct levels of each Component. So each CSS selector is looking for distinct class names and not HTML elements. This gives you more flexibility using HTML elements without worrying about them inheriting styles from something else.

"A Component is a minimal software item that can be tested in isolation."

Mark Otto wrote on his blog, **"Each class name begins with a prefix. Class name prefixing makes our code more durable and easier to maintain, but it also better enables us to scope styles to only the relevant elements."**

Dependency

If you are working on a Node.js or using Grunt/Gulp/Bower you might hear the term code Dependency or list of dependencies. What this means is your project depends on another code library or framework to function properly.

So your project lists these dependencies inside your `package.json` file and if you use Bower in a `bower.json` file.

In the example below I am using some Grunt packages in my project. When I install them I have the option of saving them as dev dependencies which essentially adds the name of the package to the package.json file.

That way if anyone downloads my project from GitHub and does an npm install command it will download everything I used when I was developing the project. Sort of like a list of ingredients for a recipe.

Markup

What does HTML Markup mean? Another name for HTML or hyper text Markup language. Commonly used to reference just the HTML or structure of the page and not the styles or scripts associated with it.

Mobile-friendly

You might have seen a little note under your website in a Google search result page saying your site is not mobile-friendly. But what does that mean? How do you make your site or web application mobile-friendly? You can test your site using this online testing tool from Google[1].

How is it Different from a Responsive Website?

Mobile-friendly is essentially the broad term for a site having a good user experience on mobile devices. The recommended method is responsive design. It is a one-size fits all approach. You could also have a dedicated mobile site or use adaptive design which loads different code depending on the device. But these options are more technical and require device detection on the server to provide the correct site version.

Pre-processor

In web design, we use a lot of CSS preprocessors like Sass, LESS, or stylus. A Preprocessor converts these raw input data and outputs regular CSS that a web browser can read and use.

But why use a Preprocessor like Sass to begin with? Well, you can think of it like a Sega CD or expansion pack shown below. Those addon devices extend the capabilities of a Sega Genesis to make it more awesome and fun to use.

---

1   https://search.google.com/test/mobile-friendly

That is essentially what Sass does for developers. It lets us write CSS in a faster more reusable way because we know it will eventually become regular CSS.

Repository or Repo

A Repo is s short name for a code repository. A collection of website files that contains a history of revisions called commits. A common place to host files using the git version control is GitHub.

Responsive Web Design

Responsive design was introduced to help designers build one site on one domain that responds to a users viewport. The two necessary elements for a responsive design are a meta viewport tag to disable scaling and media queries to alter the design of the page gets smaller. Responsive design is a lot less expensive and easier to maintain than the other mobile strategies. This has added to its rapid growth and adoption.

A big challenge with responsive design is finding a balance between the content needs for both mobile and desktop. A desktop site has a lot of visual real estate that is often filled with carousels, videos, large parallax background images, and large blocks of text. If you load a feature-rich website on a mobile device you often increase the page load for mobile visitors. This is due to the large images and videos which are scaled down to mobile.

SASS or SCSS

Sass stands for syntactically awesome stylesheets. Sass is a scripting language that is compiled into regular CSS. It was created to help writing CSS easier and more efficient.

You can create variables for colors, font-sizes, and any other value. You can then use that variable throughout your styles to make global changes without having to find and replace to make a change.

You can break up your stylesheet into subfiles like `_nav.scss`, `_typography.scss` and then merge them together into one file named `styles.css`.

You can create and use mixins which are essentially a block of styles you can insert to your rules. One way I use mixins is for fonts. Often fonts have a font-family, color, font-weight, etc that when I declare a font I want all of those properties to be applied. This saves you time maintaining all of the properties throughout your stylesheet.

User Experience - UX

When designing something you have to consider how it looks (UI) and how it functions (UX) but these two overlap a lot. Basically, the user experience considers how someone would interact with your website or application. What information do they need to succeed in their goals? How do they feel after using the site? Was it annoying or easy to follow and understand?

Knowing your user and customer is extremely important and often requires surveys, interviews, and developing a persona. This persona helps guide your design and development process to consider your user first.

User Interface - UI

UI design produces a product's skin - a product's visual/graphic presentation. It is also responsible for communicating a brand's strengths to best enhance the user's experience. In an application, it also guides the user through the interface and provides help notifications, error messages, and visual interaction feedback.

Want something else explained?

Email me with a word or concept you would like explained: https://bootstrapcreative. com/contact-us/

Web Development Reference Sites

Bootstrap Design Inspiration

- **Bootstrap Expo:** https://expo.getbootstrap.com/
- **Built With Bootstrap:** http://builtwithbootstrap.com/
- **Wrap Bootstrap:** https://wrapbootstrap.com/
- **Official Bootstrap Themes:** https://themes.getbootstrap.com/
- **AWWWARDS:** https://www.awwwards.com/websites/responsive-design/
- **Media Queries:** https://mediaqueri.es/
- **Pattern Tap:** http://zurb.com/patterntap
- **CodePen Pattern Library:** http://codepen.io/patterns/
- **Building Blocks:** http://foundation.zurb.com/building-blocks/

Bootstrap Example Library

Find Bootstrap 4 code snippets and page layout examples that will save you time. Each snippet contains a demo and the code necessary to achieve the functionality in your project.
https://bootstrapcreative.com/pattern/

HTML Reference

- **Mozilla HTML Reference:** https://developer.mozilla.org/en-US/docs/Web/HTML
- **HTMLReference.io:** http://htmlreference.io/

CSS Reference

- **Mozilla CSS Reference:** https://developer.mozilla.org/en-US/docs/Web/CSS
- **CSS-Tricks Almanac:** https://css-tricks.com/almanac/
- **Can I Use?:** http://caniuse.com/
- **CSSreference.io:** http://cssreference.io/

JavaScript Reference

- **Mozilla JavaScript Reference:** https://developer.mozilla.org/en-US/docs/Web/JavaScript
- **jQuery Documentation:** http://api.jquery.com/

Bootstrap Reference

- **Bootstrap 4 Classes Reference:** https://bootstrapcreative.com/resources/bootstrap-4-css-classes-index/
- **Official Bootstrap Documentation:** http://getbootstrap.com/
- **Bootsnip:** http://bootsnipp.com/

Responsive Images Reference Guide

One of the main causes of slow loading pages on mobile devices is large images.

HTML5 introduced two features that allow the developer to specify different sized images at different media queries. Using one of these will help your sites load quicker and improve the user experience.

<picture> Element

```
<picture>
  <source srcset="https://dummyimage.com/2000x400/000/fff" media="(min-width:
1400px)">
  <source srcset="https://dummyimage.com/1400x400/000/fff" media="(min-width:
768px)">
  <source srcset="https://dummyimage.com/800x400/000/fff" media="(min-width:
576px)">
  <img srcset="https://dummyimage.com/600x400/000/fff" alt="" class="d-block
img-fluid">
</picture>
```

The picture element[2] gives you a lot of control on how your image looks on different breakpoints and retina displays. As you resize your window the browser will load the necessary image. It takes more work up-front to build the images but the control is worth it in prominent locations like carousels. Here is a CodePen[3] of various image proportions. If you need to support IE11 and below use this polyfill.[4]

---

2   https://www.html5rocks.com/en/tutorials/responsive/picture-element/

3   https://codepen.io/JacobLett/pen/NjramL?editors=1100

4   https://scottjehl.github.io/picturefill/

If a picture looks blurry on a retina device you can add a high res img like this:

```
<source srcset="img/blog-post-1000x600-2.jpg, blog-post-1000x600-2@2x.jpg 2x"
media="(min-width: 768px)">
```

When to Use This

When you want to change how an image looks on different breakpoints (size, cropping, etc.) I commonly use them with carousels and image cards

Image srcset=""

```
<img src="https://dummyimage.com/400x200/000/fff" srcset="https://dummyimage.
com/800x400/000/fff 1000w, https://dummyimage.com/1600x600/000/fff 2000w,
https://dummyimage.com/1600x600/000/fff 2x" alt="">
```

Image srcset[5] is an attribute added to an image tag and provides various images for the browser to use depending on the viewport width. It is best used when you need little control on how it is cropped and sized. But you want to speed up page load on mobile and get rid of image pixilation on retina displays. If you need to support IE11 and below use this polyfill[6].

One challenge with this solution is that the image is loaded on page load and does not change when the browser is resized due to image caching. To work around this, I found disabling browser cache in DevTools[7] will load the new image.

---

5   https://css-tricks.com/responsive-images-youre-just-changing-resolutions-use-srcset/
6   https://scottjehl.github.io/picturefill/
7   https://stackoverflow.com/questions/5690269/disabling-chrome-cache-for-website-development

When to Use This

- Blog post images

- Any image you want to look the same (same proportions and image) but just want to increase resolution.

Summary

Both the `<picture>` element and img `srcset` will help you specify the right image size at the right time to improve the page load speed. Without this, you would be loading a large image on a mobile device. I personally prefer the picture element because it gives me the most control on exactly the image I want to display instead of leaving the decision up to the browser. Plus it makes it a lot easier to test it is working properly.

Find an error?
Or have a comment?

Contact support@bootstrapcreative.com

Save Time Using Bootstrap 4

Get the Bootstrap 4 Toolkit

Includes project starter templates, tutorial videos, and reference guides.

https://bootstrapcreative.com/b4toolkit